CIVIL WAR MEDICINE

- An Illustrated History -

Mark J. Schaadt, M.D.

CEDARWOOD PUBLISHING

Quincy, Illinois

Published by:
Cedarwood Publishing
1907 Cedarwood Lane
Quincy, IL 62301

Printed by:
JK Creative Printers
2029 Hollister Whitney Parkway
Quincy, IL 62301

LIBRARY OF CONGRESS
CATALOG CARD NUMBER 98-92995

ISBN 0-9664768-0-8

Printed in the United States of America

Second Printing - May, 2000

– Table of Contents –

- Illustrations -

- Preface & Acknowledgments -

It is estimated that there have been more than 50,000 books written on the subject of the American Civil War. If these books had been written during the four year time period of the war itself, this volume of literature would require the publication of nearly 35 books per day, every day of the war. Subjects of these books include any conceivable topic pertaining to the conflict; the causes of the war, the battles fought, the weapons used, the generals, the soldiers, and the politicians.

Within this massive volume of work are approximately 20 - 30 titles that deal primarily with the medical aspects of the Civil War. Several are excellent, and many were used for reference in the preparation of this book. The purpose of this book is to provide a general overview of the medical and surgical aspects of the Civil War. Topics covered include the political aspects of the Union and Confederate Medical Departments, medical personnel - including physicians, nurses, and other ancillary staff, and actual medical and surgical practices of the war. This book includes numerous references to medical texts and other materials available at the time of the war, statistics tabulated after the war, and information obtained from recent works. Many illustrations and photographs are also included.

In an effort to prevent constant referral to a glossary, I have attempted to define medical and technical terms within the body of the text. Terms not defined may be found in any standard dictionary.

I would like to thank the various authors and publishers who gave permission to use material from their books. Please note references and comments in the bibliography. Without these works, this book would not have been possible. I would especially like to thank Norman Publishing, and Gordon Dammann, D.D.S. Thanks also to Dr. Dammann for providing the photograph of Dr. Samuel Everett.

Thanks to Dorcas Recks and Arlis Dittmer, the librarians in the medical library at Blessing Hospital in Quincy, IL, for obtaining copies of articles from the medical journal, *The Military Surgeon*, from the early 1900's, as well as other helpful information.

Thanks to the Illinois State Historical Library in Springfield, IL, for providing access to *The Medical and Surgical History of the War of the Rebellion* (and the reprinted version; *The Medical and Surgical History of the Civil War*) and *The Documents of the U.S. Sanitary Commission*.

Thanks to JK Creative Printers of Quincy, IL, and their President, Gail Henderson, for the excellent job they did in printing the book.

Thanks to my parents, Cyril and Patricia Schaadt, for a lifetime of support and encouragement.

Most of all, thanks to my wife, Kristin, for putting up with my time-consuming habit of reading or watching anything related to the Civil War, my expensive hobby of collecting Civil War medical items, and my time-consuming *and* expensive project of writing this book.

Mark Schaadt
May, 1998

Through these fields of destruction
Baptisms of fire
I've watched all your suffering
As the battle raged higher
And though they did hurt me so bad
In the fear and alarm
you did not desert me
My brothers in arms

From the song, Brothers in Arms
Performed by Dire Straits
Lyrics by Mark Knopfler
Copyright © 1988 Phonogram Ltd. (London)

- PROLOGUE -

Samuel W. Everett, M.D. was forty years old when the Civil War began in 1861. Dr. Everett was a physician in Quincy, Illinois, a bustling river town located in west-central Illinois, situated high on a bluff overlooking the Mississippi river.

The Everett family had lived in Quincy since 1840, when Samuel's father, Charles, moved his family from London, England to the United States. Samuel became a prominent and respected physician in the community. One of Samuel's brothers, Edward, became a well-known scholar and public speaker. Edward is perhaps best known for the two hour oration he performed on November 19, 1863; the "opening act" to Lincoln's three minute Gettysburg Address.

Samuel lived in Quincy with his twenty-nine year old wife, Mary, and their one year old son, Henry.

Dr. Everett was running a successful medical practice when the opening guns were fired at Fort Sumpter on April 12, 1861. Living just across the river from the slave state of Missouri, anti-slavery and anti-secession sentiments ran high throughout the community. Dr. Everett responded to Lincoln's initial call for volunteers, and on April 29, 1861, he enlisted as the Regimental Surgeon for the 10th Illinois Infantry.

He reported to Cairo, Illinois, the location of headquarters for the Western Department of the Union Army. Apparently showing significant medical and leadership skills, he was promoted to the position of Brigade Surgeon of the 2nd Division, on the staff of Major General John Pope, in September, 1861. In October, he was appointed Medical Director of the 2nd Division of the Army of the West. Dr. Everett was assigned to staff duty at the U.S. Army's Fourth Street General Hospital in St. Louis, Missouri.

In March, 1862, Dr. Everett was ordered to leave St. Louis and report for duty to the headquarters of the Army of the Tennessee, under the command of Major General Ulysses S. Grant, located three miles from Pittsburg Landing, Tennessee. He was assigned the position of Brigade Surgeon for the 6th Division, under the command of General Benjamin Prentiss, another Quincy native.

On April 6, 1862, the Union Army, under the command of General Grant, met the Confederate Army, under the command of General Albert Sidney Johnston. The two armies clashed near the crossroads at Shiloh Church, about two miles southwest of Pittsburg Landing. Between 12:30 p.m. and 6:30 p.m., Prentiss and his men repelled eleven massed Confederate assaults in an area now known as the Hornet's Nest - due to the sound made by hundreds of musket balls as they whizzed through the trees.

Dr. Everett stayed with his men, working as they were fighting. The sights and sounds must have been horrifying, as he tried to attend to injured soldiers during the heat of the battle.

Then - suddenly - it was all over. One line in the voluminous "*Medical and Surgical History of the War of the Rebellion*" states, very succinctly, "Battle of Shiloh. Samuel W. Everett. Brigade Surgeon. Killed instantly by a ball striking him in the forehead."

For Dr. Everett, the Civil War ended on April 6, 1862, in the smoky woods near Shiloh Church, Tennessee; three hundred miles from his home, his wife, and his son. A family doctor who paid the ultimate price in the service of his country.

More than twelve thousand surgeons would eventually serve in the Union army. Thirty-two would die on the battlefield. Dr. Samuel W. Everett was the first.

Dr. Samuel W. Everett

Between the years of 1861 and 1865, America was at war with itself.
The American Civil War would produce some gruesome statistics.

Of the nearly 3 million soldiers who participated in the conflict, approximately 618,000 would die. Roughly two-thirds, or 400,000, would die by disease. One-third, or 200,000, would die in battle, or from wounds sustained in battle. Of this total, the Union lost 359,528; the Confederacy, about 258,000. This loss to the Confederacy represented the death of one out of every four men of military age.

The total mortality figure of the war represents the loss of 2 % of the entire U.S. population at that time. In terms of today's U.S. population, this would represent the loss of 5 million young, able-bodied men.

Not reflected in the mortality statistics is the incalculable suffering of men wounded or struck down by illness. Union statistics document the treatment of almost a half million injuries and 6 million cases of illness. Approximately 50,000 amputations were performed in the North and South combined. Nearly a half million men came out of the war permanently disabled. Many more endured significant pain and hardship long after the war had ended. The tens of thousands of disabled soldiers at home with missing limbs, disfiguring injuries, and chronic illnesses, would be a daily reminder of the terrible cost of the war. A reminder that would last for years.

It is all too easy to become lost in these mind-numbing statistics. In reality, each and every one of those young men was a son, a brother, a husband, a relative, a friend. By 1865, there could not have been an individual or family that was not touched by pain and loss.

"War is all Hell"
William Tecumseh Sherman

BACKGROUND

One cannot truly understand the medical aspects of the American Civil War without being aware of two important concepts. First, the Civil War was, in some respects, the first "modern war" in terms of military technology - armies could inflict huge numbers of casualties in very short periods of time. Second, basic medical theory and surgical practice had remained relatively unchanged for hundreds of years.

The evolution of military tactics had not kept pace with considerable "improvements" in technology. Technological advancements first available during the Civil War included (1) the telegraph for rapid communication between generals, their staffs, and the government; facilitating the coordination of the military effort over a large area, (2) the availability of a well-developed railroad system for movement of large numbers of troops and supplies, and, most significantly, (3) the development of the rifled musket and minie ball. These technological advances were coupled with obsolete military strategy and tactics taught in leading military academies. Most generals, on both sides, were schooled in the tactics of the "Napoleanic charge" (massed volley fire by troops at extremely close range), and many had fought in the Mexican war (1846-1848) armed with smooth bore muskets. The Model 1816 .69 caliber smooth bore musket fires a round ball projectile down a smooth bore barrel. This projectile is accurate at hitting a man-sized target at 50 yards. Accuracy falls off considerably between 50 and 100 yards.[1] The cylindro-conoidal "minie" ball was developed by French Captain Claude E. Minie, and was adopted by the U.S Army in 1852. The Model 1861 rifled musket fires a .58 caliber minie ball down a rifled barrel, scored with a spiral groove, which imparts spin to the bullet as it leaves the barrel, greatly extending range and improving accuracy. This cone-shaped, soft lead projectile weighs about one ounce, and flattens and deforms on impact, causing significant damage to soft tissues and bony structures. This bullet could accurately hit a man-sized target at 500 yards, with accuracy falling off between 500 and 1000 yards.[2] Both the smooth bore and rifled muskets are muzzle-loading weapons. Under ideal conditions a soldier might get off three shots per minute, usually much less. With the smooth bore musket accurate to 50 yards, a massed assault against a defensive position was subjected to only one or two volleys of fire before the defensive position could be overrun. With the longer effective range of the rifled musket, soldiers were subjected to fire over much greater distances as they approached defensive works; turning massed assaults into suicidal charges.

The second key concept is the embryonic stage that medical knowledge was in at the time of the Civil War. There was very little academic medicine in the United States. Most medical researchers were working in places like France, Austria, Germany, and England. Dissemination of medical knowledge was hindered by political rivalries. Trans-oceanic communication was difficult, and information and ideas were rarely shared. The concepts that would later lead to our knowledge of infectious disease were in their infancy in the early 1860's, and researchers were often the subjects of scorn and ridicule by opinionated and influential traditional practitioners.

Significant work being performed at the time included that of Austrian physician, Ignaz Semmelweis, who in 1848 practically eliminated puerpural fever from the obstetrical clinic in Vienna. This often fatal infection had long been thought to be due to over-crowding, poor ventilation, the onset of lactation, or "miasma" (foul odors or vapors in the air). In general, most of the diseases we now know to be infectious in etiology were felt to be caused by these types of factors. Semmelweis noted that the patients of mid-wives, who traditionally washed their hands between deliveries, did not contract puerperal fever, whereas his own medical students, who would go from patient to patient without handwashing, had high incidences of the disease. He subsequently required his students to wash their hands in a chlorinated lime solution between patients, and the disease was virtually eliminated. Semmelweis became active in the Vienna political revolution of 1848-1849. The revolution was put down and Semmelweis was fired from his position. His medical opinions were ridiculed and unaccepted by the academic medical community. He published his work in 1861, but it was rejected. He suffered a mental breakdown and died in 1865. The tremendous importance of his work would not be recognized until after his death.[3]

Another avid researcher was France's Louis Pasteur. His studies of fermentation and food spoilage led to many of the fundamental concepts of microbiology. In 1857, he proposed that fermentation was the result of the activity of minute organisms. His work in identifying the bacterial cause of certain diseases, such as anthrax, did not occur until the late 1860's-1870's.[4]

Joseph Lister, an English surgeon (1827-1912), can rightly be considered the father of modern surgical antisepsis. His father helped develop the modern microscope, undoubtedly exposing Joseph to the concepts of microbiology early in his life. In the early 1860's, he rejected the popular concept of the miasmatic cause of illness, and postulated that infection and sepsis might be caused by dust-like substances in the air. There is no evidence that he believed this "dust" to be a living organism. He became acquainted with the work of Pasteur in 1865, and began to combine the ideas of infectious organisms and wound contamination. In August, 1865 (four months after the end of the Civil War), he began the practice of cleaning his hands and surgical instruments with a dilute solution of carbolic acid. In 1867, Lister published his landmark work, "*On the Antiseptic Principle in the Practice of Surgery.*" Between 1865 and 1869, the mortality rate in his surgical ward dropped from 45% to 15%. As usual, physicians in practice were resistant to accepting his new ideas. Lister's coup-de-grace came in 1877, when, using his antiseptic technique, he surgically opened a fractured kneecap, wired the pieces together, and closed the wound. Never before had a surgeon purposely opened a fracture, thereby exposing the bone to contamination. There was no evidence of post-operative infection, and the fracture healed perfectly. The era of modern surgery had begun - twelve years too late for the Civil War soldier.[5]

In 1861, the lack of knowledge regarding the infectious cause of illness also resulted in an almost complete absence of basic hygienic and sanitation principles. Soldiers lived in large, crowded camps, where food and water were contaminated by fecal material from the men and their horses. In close quarters, common infectious illnesses ran rampant. Medical therapies of the day were based on antiquated medical theory that did not take into account the infectious causes of disease.

One can only wonder as to how many fewer men would have died, if the surgeons had practiced the simple act of hand and instrument washing, as they treated patient after patient, and performed amputation after amputation, or had used clean water and sponges as they washed wounds and changed dressings. Countless cases of illness could have been prevented by using basic hygienic practices.

Without knowledge of the infectious causes of disease, these well-meaning surgeons contributed greatly to the mortality of the Civil War.

———————————————————————

PART 1

THE MEDICAL DEPARTMENT:

POLITICS,
ORGANIZATION,
AND
PERSONNEL

In 1861, the Medical Department of the U.S. Army was totally unprepared for a war that would produce the numbers and types of casualties that the Civil War was about to provide. Never before (or since) had the American continent seen a conflict of this magnitude. The existing military and civilian medical systems were completely inadequate to handle the thousands upon thousands of casualties that would soon be rolling in. The ability to make the system work, and provide adequate medical care to these ill and injured soldiers, would require extensive revision, adaptation, and improvisation. These changes and adaptations would take place at several levels; in the federal government's Medical Department, in the civilian effort to help provide medical supplies and police the overall provision of medical care, and in the task of providing the military with the thousands of physicians it would soon require to actually provide this care.

For the Confederacy, the task was even more daunting; they were starting from scratch.

I - POLITICS

The U.S. Surgeon General, in 1861, was Colonel Thomas Lawson, a veteran of the War of 1812. He was over eighty years of age at the outbreak of the Civil War. Lawson was first and foremost a politician, concerned primarily with budgetary matters. Supplies were kept to a minimum and medical staff numbers were low. Lawson had little regard for the quality of medical service provided, as long as it was cheap. He did not tolerate criticism of his department, and was not open to suggestions for improvement. Within a month, however, Colonel Lawson became seriously ill, and was temporarily replaced by Surgeon R.C. Wood. Wood was more receptive to the actual medical needs of the soldiers, and was willing to critically examine the inadequacies of the Medical Department. Unlike Lawson, he was receptive to suggestions for improvement in medical care, that were being vocalized by citizen groups such as the U.S. Sanitary Commission. He went so far as to recommend to the government that a civilian commission of "inquiry and advice" be created to work along with the Medical Department.[6]

Lawson's death, in June, 1861, resulted in the appointment of the senior surgeon of the Army, Dr. Clement A. Finley, to the position of Surgeon General. Dr. Finley was in his sixties at the time of his appointment. With his endorsement, a civilian medical advisory board, the United States Sanitary Commission, was authorized on June 13th. The first major battle of the Civil War, Bull Run, occurred on July 21th. The Medical Department was unprepared for the tremendous number of casualties this battle would produce. Wounded soldiers were left unattended, on the battlefield, for hours. Ambulance service was essentially nonexistent, and many of the wounded walked, or were carried back, to

Washington, D.C., thirty miles from the battlefield. Regimental surgeons would often treat only the soldiers from their own regiments, and refuse to treat others. The inadequate treatment of these wounded soldiers was criticized by military personnel and civilians alike. Dr. Finley proved to be much less receptive to outside suggestions than was originally hoped, and communication and cooperation between the Sanitary Commission and the Medical Department soon became impossible. The Medical Department continued to run short on supplies, short on staff, and appeared to be totally lacking in foresight and preparation. It was immediately clear that, in order to provide an acceptable level of medical care, the system would have to be reorganized from the top down.

Frederick Law Olmstead, the executive secretary of the Sanitary Commission, perhaps said it best in terms of the previous Surgeon General appointments: "It is a criminal weakness to entrust such responsibilities...to a self-satisfied, supercilious, bigoted blockhead, merely because he is the oldest of the old messroom doctors of the frontier guard of the country. He knows nothing and does nothing, and is capable of knowing nothing and doing nothing, but quibble about matters of form and precedent."[7] and whose principal occupation "is to sign his name to papers which require that ceremony before they can be admitted to eternal rest in the pigeonholes of the bureau."[8]

In 1862, the Secretary of War, Simon Cameron was replaced by Edwin Stanton. He met almost immediately with representatives of the Sanitary Commission and became convinced "of an urgent necessity of reorganizing and remodeling the Medical Bureau." Congress passed a reorganization bill on April 16, 1862. The bill provided for a Surgeon General, a Sanitary Inspector General, and a number of Sanitary Inspectors. All appointments would be based on merit, given higher military rank, and all would be under sixty years of age.[9]

Stanton also meant to improve the general caliber of surgeon deemed acceptable for duty. In 1862, he dismissed an incompetent medical officer stating, "A negligent or inhuman surgeon is regarded by this Department as an enemy of his country, and of his race; and will be dealt with according to the utmost rigor of the military law."[10]

Surgeon General Finely was removed from office. Dr. William Hammond was endorsed by the Sanitary Commission to be his replacement. Hammond had been a long-time army physician, and was a friend of General George B. McClellan. On April 25, 1862, Hammond was appointed Surgeon General. Born in 1828, he was 33 years old at the time of his appointment. He began his study of medicine at age 16, and graduated from the Medical Department of the University of New York in 1848, at the age of 20. He entered the Medical Department of the Army in 1849.[11]

Hammond immediately began to perform. His attitude regarding his new position can be summed up by his statement, "The saving of money was altogether a secondary object. My first duty was to save life."[12] He secured an increase in personnel for the Medical Corps, produced better reports, provided plentiful supplies, built improved hospitals on a large scale, initiated a hired hospital corps for the general hospitals, founded the beginnings of an army medical museum, and a medical history of the war. He recommended an ambulance corps, a permanent military general hospital, and an army medical school.[13] He demanded that his department take over from the Quartermaster Corps the control of the ambulances, the medical supply trains, and the construction of military hospitals.[14]

Not the least of his actions was his appointment of Surgeon Jonathan Letterman, as Medical Director for the Army of the Potomac. Letterman would eventually devise, and put into effect, an efficient and effective ambulance system, a field supply system, and a field hospital system.[15]

Unfortunately, the job of Surgeon General was political, and Dr. Hammond was not a very "political" man. He lacked tack and diplomacy. Stanton and Hammond started out as friends but somehow became enemies. The exact reasons for the rift that developed between them are unknown but more than likely involved a basic personality conflict. Both men were somewhat self-centered and domineering, causing them to clash in most of their interactions. In August, 1863, Hammond was ordered to New Orleans to personally attend to matters concerning the South Atlantic and Gulf medical departments.[16]

In Hammond's absence, Surgeon Joseph K. Barnes was named acting Surgeon General in Washington. Dr. Barnes had been in Washington since May, 1862, and was the personal physician of Secretary of War Stanton and many officers in the city. He was well-liked by his superiors and subordinates alike. Like Hammond before him, he also had become personal friends with Stanton and the two seemed to have genuinely gotten along. Hammond did not get back to Washington until December, 1863, and he was sent immediately to Chattanooga and Nashville, to attend to Medical Department concerns there. The run-around had begun. His enemies in Washington began a search of his records to look for political ammunition against him. Hammond repeatedly requested permission to return to Washington and was repeatedly denied. Around Christmas, 1863, Hammond was injured in a fall, and was transferred to Washington for treatment on January 15, 1864.[17] Barnes continued in his role as acting Surgeon General, over the protests of Hammond.

1864 was an election year in Washington. George McClellan had been replaced as the General of the Army. He was now running against Lincoln for the presidency and his friends and supporters in Washington were being politically destroyed. Surgeon General Hammond was one of McClellan's friends and political allies. Hammond, justifiably angry over his treatment, demanded a hearing, to get all the facts into the open, on both sides. Considering the political climate at the time, it is no surprise that the deck was stacked against him from the start. Flimsy charges were drawn up and a trial scheduled. Stanton was friend and political ally to the Judge Advocate, as well as every single member of the court. The court met for the first time on January 19, 1864 and the trial lasted nearly four months. In May, the record went to Judge Advocate General Bingham for review. Hammond was found guilty on a number of charges involving such things as improper purchasing arrangements, purchasing excessive quantities of supplies, purchasing supplies of inferior quality, and showing preference to certain dealers. His sentence was: "To be dismissed from the service and to be forever disqualified from holding any office of profit or trust under the Government of the United States."[18]

Hammond was out; Dr. Joseph K. Barnes was in. It has been said of Hammond's tenure in office that, " ...his successor originated nothing more, asked for nothing more; merely kept the Hammond machine moving."[19] Barnes' reputation is based on the establishment of the Army Medical Museum, the Army Medical Library, and the publication, after the war, of the initial volumes of the "*Medical and Surgical History of the War of the Rebellion*." Each of these had been initiated by Surgeon General Hammond. For the remainder of the war, the administration of the duties of the Medical Department changed very little from the Hammond regime.[20]

Hammond moved to New York City, where he became an authority on nervous and mental diseases. He lectured in several medical schools and was a great success, both professionally and financially. In 1878, Hammond attempted to clear his name by having his Civil War case reviewed before Congress. Hammond specifically requested political and personal vindication; no financial compensation. The case was reviewed, and a bill was introduced into the Senate and the House seeking reversal of the Civil War verdict. It passed both legislative bodies and was approved by the President of the United States. The Civil War trial proceedings and sentence were annulled, and William A. Hammond's name was placed on the retired list of the Army on August 27,1879.[21]

Unfortunately, most of the records pertaining to the Confederate Medical Department were destroyed with the burning of Richmond in April, 1865. This tragic loss results in a paucity of details in regards to many aspects of Civil War medicine, from the Confederate perspective.

The first Confederate Surgeon General was Dr. David DeLeon. He held this position for about 2 months. The second Surgeon General, Dr. Charles Smith, lasted about 2 weeks. On July 30, 1861, Dr. Samuel Preston Moore was appointed to the position. Moore would preside as Surgeon General for the remainder of the war. A native of South Carolina, Moore had been a surgeon in the regular U.S. Army, and was one of twenty-four physicians in the U.S. Army who had resigned and gone to the South at the outbreak of hostilities. Moore's military history included service in the Mexican War. The Medical Department operated very efficiently under his guidance. He worked hard to insure that competent physicians held key positions. Surgeons were required to undergo professional examinations to confirm knowledge and skill. A medical board was authorized to screen potential candidates and perform disciplinary action if necessary. He encouraged the accumulation of data for comparison purposes, and endorsed clinical discussions and publications concerning medical topics of importance. More than likely, this information would have been published, after the war, in a similar fashion to the Union's "*Medical and Surgical History of the War of the Rebellion,*" but the loss of the Confederate Medical Department's records made this impossible. Among his other achievements, Moore was also responsible for significant improvements in the structure and function of hospitals. It is claimed that he is responsible for the introduction of the general pavilion hospital, the forerunner of the modern hospital of today; where patients with similar illnesses or injuries are grouped together in wards. Instead of housing patients in large multi-story buildings, the pavilion hospital consisted of individual one story wards or huts. This resulted in better access to patients, better ventilation, and the segregation of patients according to their type of illness or injury, allowing for specialized care.[22] This arrangement was adopted in Northern general hospitals as well.

II - MEDICAL DEPARTMENT ORGANIZATION

<u>U.S. Medical Department</u>

The U.S. Medical Department (or Bureau), in January, 1861, consisted of the Surgeon General, 30 surgeons, and 83 assistant surgeons. At the outbreak of war, 3 surgeons and 21 assistant surgeons resigned to side with the South.[23] Hundreds of civilian doctors enlisted as regimental surgeons and assistant surgeons, joining volunteer regiments, usually mustered-in near their home towns. Like the colonels of these regiments, the surgeons were appointed by the governors of their states. These appointments often had nothing to do with medical knowledge or surgical expertise. These physicians were, for the most part, local "country" doctors. They had little or no surgical experience and had never been exposed to wartime casualties. Their training would be on the job. The government also hired many civilian surgeons to staff the growing number of general hospitals. These "contract surgeons" also had varying levels of skill and experience. Examination procedures were inconsistent and varied state to state. Scrutiny became even more lax as more surgeons were needed. The first regiments that responded to Lincoln's initial call for volunteers - after the firing on Fort Sumpter in April, 1861 - supplied their own surgeons. At that time, there were no federal regulations and many felt that some of these surgeons were of very dubious quality. In May, with a call for another 40 regiments, each regiment was required to have one surgeon and one assistant surgeon, commissioned by the governor of the state, and each having successfully passed a state examination. Again, these standards were not consistently practiced. In June, 1861, the editor of a leading medical journal complained, "we may estimate by hundreds the number of unqualified persons who have received the endorsement of these medical examining boards as capable surgeons and assistant surgeons of regiments. Indeed, these examinations have in some cases been so conducted to prove the merest farce. Whoever has examined the list of surgeons, passed by the different state examining committees, must have regretted to find so few names of eminent surgeons."[24] This statement should not be misconstrued to insinuate that all Civil War surgeons were incompetent. Several states had rigorous examinations and produced many surgeons that stood out for their competence. These states included Ohio, Vermont, and Massachusetts. As the war progressed, and surgeons gained experience - often very rapidly, treating large numbers of cases - their expertise improved. Surgeons that could make the grade were respected by their staffs and troops; those that could not, moved on.

Eventually, the U.S. Army was to have approximately 12,000 doctors on its payroll. Full-time surgeons were paid $165.00 per month and ranked as majors. Assistant surgeons were ranked as captains or first lieutenants and received $100.00 or $130.00 per month. Assistant surgeons could become surgeons and surgeons could rise to administrative positions that made them lieutenant colonels or colonels.[25]

By April, 1865, the surgeons had been organized into seven bodies:[26]

1- Surgeons and Assistant Surgeons of the U.S. Army. This was the regular Medical Corps, composed of men in service when the war began and such additions as Congress had authorized. Once the war was under way they were used for staff duty.

2- Surgeons and Assistant Surgeons of Volunteers. Created by Congress to supplement the work of the Regulars in staff duty. There were 547 such commissions issued. This catagory included the former "Brigade Surgeons."

3- Regimental Surgeons and Assistant Surgeons. Commissioned by state governors rather than by the President. This, the largest category, numbered 2,109 Surgeons and 3,882 Assistant Surgeons. This group provided the majority of care in field hospitals.

4- Acting Assistant Surgeons, U.S. Army. This included the majority of the "contract" surgeons, who held no commission but received the pay of first lieutenants. They numbered 5,532 and were employed chiefly in general hospitals, where many were engaged in private practice as well. This group provided the majority of care in the general hospitals.

5- Medical Officers of the Veteran Corps. Staff positions designated near the end of the war.

6- Acting Staff Surgeons. Staff positions designated near the end of the war.

7- Surgeons and Assistant Surgeons of Colored Troops.

Confederate Medical Department
   The organization of the newly-formed Confederate Medical Department ran along similar lines to that of the U.S. Medical Department.
   The Medical Department of the Regular Army of the Confederate States of America was authorized by the Provisional Congress at Montgomery, Alabama, on February 26, 1861, in the "Act for the Establishment and Organization of a General Staff for the Army of the Confederate States of America." This measure provided for a Medical Department consisting of one Surgeon General, four surgeons, and six assistant surgeons. As in the North, the Surgeon General was appointed to be responsible for the administration of the Medical Department. His responsibilities included, "the administrative details of the medical department, the government of hospitals, the regulation of the duties of surgeons and assistant surgeons, and the appointment of acting medical officers, when needed, for local or detached service."[27]
   Future Surgeon General, Dr. Samuel Preston Moore - along with two other surgeons and 21 assistant surgeons who came with him from the U.S. Medical Department - formed the core staff of the Confederate Medical Department. In a short period of time, these numbers were to prove inadequate and additional staff was added.
   In March, the President was authorized to appoint one surgeon and one assistant surgeon for each regiment. As in the North, these surgeons were generally local doctors, practicing in the same towns where their regiments were recruited.

The Confederate Surgeon General was ranked as colonel, surgeons as majors, and assistant surgeons as captains. Depending on length of service, surgeon's pay was between $162.00 and $200.00 a month, and assistant surgeon's pay between $110.00 and $150.00.[28] Exact numbers, in terms of Confederate medical personnel are lacking, but there were approximately 3,300 Surgeons and Assistant Surgeons approved for duty. This number does not include "contract" surgeons, data on which are lacking. The Confederacy probably utilized a total of approximately 8,000 doctors during the course of the war.

There was a hierarchical chain of command in the medical organization of the armies, both North and South. At the top of the pyramid, and responsible for the overall delivery of medical care, was the Surgeon General, who reported directly to the President. Reporting to the Surgeon General, was the medical director appointed to each army.

Initially, every brigade of an army was assigned a brigade surgeon, who reported to the appropriate medical director. The brigade surgeon was responsible for the day-to-day medical care provided to the soldiers in his brigade. Under his direction, were all the regimental surgeons, assistant surgeons, hospital stewards, and nurses. The brigade surgeons were to make camp inspections, maintain medical supplies, transmit the weekly morbidity reports of the regimental surgeons, supply casualty reports after an action, and train men for stretcher detail. In times of need, the brigade surgeon might be called upon to perform actual surgical duties or medical care. Later in the war, the functions of the brigade surgeon were performed by an appointed division or corps surgeon.

At the base of the pyramid, the regimental surgeon and their assistant surgeons provided the routine surgical and medical care for their regiment. They reported to the appropriate brigade, division, or corps surgeon.

The Medical Departments of the Union and Confederate Armies had equivalent functions and responsibilities. Each Department was presented with the same range of diseases and injuries, and their approach to the provision of medical care, from the battlefield to the general hospital, was nearly identical. Individual differences pertained more to the availability of instruments, quality and quantity of supplies, and access to various medications, rather than any particular difference in actual medical or surgical practice.

III - DOCTORS

Medical training in the United States, at the time of the Civil War, was not the structured and standardized educational process that it is today. There was a great deal of variability in the path that any given individual might have taken to become a physician. Well into the 1820's or 1830's, most physicians had not attended medical school. A person wishing to become a physician would apprentice himself to a medical practitioner, and over a period of a year or two would receive on-the-job training in the practitioner's office. When the supervising physician felt his student had obtained an adequate fund of medical knowledge and experience, the student was sent out to start his own practice. However, by the 1860's, most of the doctors who practiced medicine during the Civil War had actually attended medical school and received some degree of formal education. The founding of medical schools in the United States began around 1800, and nearly 100 medical schools were in existence by the time of the Civil War. Medical school consisted of a series of lectures covering various topics. The student attended this set of lectures over a period of one year. During the second year of medical school, he listened to the same series of lectures again. Throughout this two year period, the student obtained practical experience by being apprenticed to a practicing physician. After the second year, the student would begin medical practice, or spend more time in lectures and/or apprenticeship. Eventually, the student would receive a medical diploma. These diplomas represented vast differences in education, skill, and experience. There was no standardization of testing among medical schools, and licensing requirements and testing varied state by state.

Considering the overall level of medical knowledge at the time, a doctor's formal education, in terms of basic medical theory, may not have been all that important. Surgical expertise would become the defining skill of the Civil War physician. Civilian doctors had little surgical experience. Civilian surgery was limited to what would be very minor procedures by Civil War standards. These might include tooth extractions, laceration repair, drainage of abscesses, foreign body removal, and the like. Orthopedic practice was essentially limited to splinting. A body cavity or joint space was never to be entered. True surgery was limited to a few obstetrical and gynecological procedures. Considering the fact that many states had laws preventing medical students from dissecting cadavers, many Civil War physicians had never even seen internal organs, splintered bones, or other major trauma until their first battle experience. None would be prepared for the carnage that was to be presented to them. That experience would only come with time.

The vast majority of Civil War surgeons had been civilian physicians in general medical practice. Other than the very few who had been doctors in the U.S. Army, none had had particular training in the specifics of military medicine. In a very short period of time, they needed to achieve expertise in, primarily, two aspects of medicine. One was in the area of surgical practice, and the other in the subject of diseases commonly present in military camps.

In the 1860's, medical practice was not divided into the specialties of internal medicine and surgery as it is today. Every physician was expected to treat medical and surgical cases.

In an effort to educate these physicians in topics of relevance to military medical practice, a number of texts, pamphlets, and other educational materials were produced by medical authors on both sides of the conflict.

Informative pamphlets were produced by the U.S. Sanitary Commission. Printed for the use of medical personnel in the North, they landed in the hands of Southern practitioners as well.

Several military medical textbooks were available at the outbreak of the Civil War. Most of these textbooks had been written by European authors. Many had been written as a result of the Crimean War (1854-1856). Texts that were often cited by subsequent American writers were, "*Notes on the Surgery of the War in the Crimea; with Remarks on the Treatment of Gunshot Wounds,*" by Dr. George H. B. Macleod, "*Principles of Military Surgery,*" by Dr. John Hennen, "*Outlines of Military Surgery,*" by Sir George Ballingall, and "*Treatise on Gunshot Wounds,*" by T. Longmore.

A vast amount of information was disseminated in the form of medical texts written during the Civil War itself. Throughout the course of the Civil War, more than twenty medical texts were written by American authors, mostly surgeons and medical professors, from both the North and South. Most of these concerned the subject of surgery in reference to military injuries. A few were written about hygienic matters, or the recognition and treatment of disease.

Some of the more popular Union texts included, "*Handbook for the Military Surgeon,*" by C.S. Tripler and G.C. Blackman (Blackman finished this text when Tripler was called to Washington, in 1861, to become Medical Director of the Army of the Potomac), "*A Manual of Military Surgery,*" by S.D. Gross, "*A Practical Treatise on Military Surgery,*" by F.H. Hamilton, and "*Hand-book of Surgical Operations,*" by S. Smith.

Confederate texts included, "*A Manual of Military Surgery, Prepared for the Use of the Confederate States Army,*" by Confederate Surgeon General, S.P. Moore, "*A Manual of Military Surgery,*" by J.J. Chisolm, and "*A Epitome of Practical Surgery for Field and Hospital,*" by E. Warren.

Other useful texts written during the war included, "*Outlines of the Chief Camp Diseases of the United States Armies,*" by Joseph J. Woodward, M.D., and "*The Hospital Steward's Manual,*" by the same author.

Medical journals and periodicals were published throughout the war. In the North were "*The American Medical Times*", "*The Medical and Surgical Reporter*", and "*The Sanitary Commission Bulletin.*"

In the South, the publication of medical journals was suspended at the outbreak of war. Supplies, manpower, and equipment were all lacking. However, in 1864, the "*Confederate States Medical and Surgical Journal*" began circulation.[29]

Various medical societies held meetings, military medicine conferences convened in large cities, and information regarding new medical theories and surgical procedures was disseminated in print and by word of mouth.

In time, the pre-war civilian medical practitioner became a Civil War surgeon. Those with good surgical skills performed the vast number of operations in field hospitals and general hospitals. Those with less surgical expertise were responsible for record-keeping, sick-call, minor surgeries, and treatment of ill soldiers. A certain amount of technical material was learned from textbooks, pamphlets, and other literature, but the vast amount of learning came from experience. The Civil War produced an endless stream of patients on which the surgeon could refine his skills.

IV - CIVILIAN ORGANIZATIONS

It did not take long for military personnel and civilians on both sides of the conflict to realize that neither government, Union nor Confederate, was prepared to provide an acceptable level of medical care to the ill or injured soldier. Initially, the governments were not receptive to civilian ideas or involvement in what they considered to be purely military business.

In the North, the concept of medical assistance from civilian organizations came from two different factions, and organization began shortly after the firing on Fort Sumpter, in April, 1861.

First, there were various women's organizations, usually formed by the mothers, sisters, or wives of soldiers in the army. They got together to make clothing, underwear, bandages, lint for dressings, hospital gowns, hospital bedding, and so forth. These groups formed under names such as "Soldier's Aid Societies" or "Ladies Aid Societies."[30]

Secondly, several prominent medical professionals of the day hoped to prevent the horrors that occurred during the last similar conflict; the Crimean War of 1854-1856. From that war, medical records had been accumulated, casualty statistics had been compiled, and several medical articles and texts had been written by surgeons involved in the conflict. The story they told was not good. Sanitary conditions were appalling. Food shortages often pushed troops to the point of starvation. Medical supplies and equipment were severely lacking and of poor quality. Transportation of the wounded from the battlefield was never sufficiently organized and hospital conditions were deplorable. The mortality rate of the Crimean War was almost 30%. That is, out of every 1000 soldiers involved in the conflict, nearly 300 died of illness or injury. A group of civilian doctors and other professionals wanted to provide their thoughts on how to prevent a similar disaster in the impending conflict. The Rev. Henry W. Bellows, a prominent Unitarian minister and pastor of All Souls Unitarian Church in New York, and Dr. Elisha Harris, a leading New York physician, formed the nucleus of this group.[31~32]

On April 29, 1861, Dr. Elizabeth Blackwell, the first woman physician in the United States, organized a meeting of socially prominent women at the Cooper Institute in New York City. They formed the Women's Central Relief Association. Rev. Bellows and Dr. Harris became officers in this organization.[33]

On May 18th, a delegation from the Women's Central Relief Association, along with members from two other similar organizations, went to Washington to meet with the Secretary of War and the Surgeon General. They lobbied for the approval of a civilian organization, the United States Sanitary Commission, to assist in the provision and monitoring of medical care during the war.

Areas they were particularly interested in included; better examination of recruits, the training of cooks, provision of female nurses to Army hospitals, the hiring of orderlies to assist with wound dressings, and an ambulance service. They wanted to ensure provision of adequate food, clothing, tents, and sanitary facilities. Basic hygienic principles were high on their list of concerns. They wanted the right to inspect hospital facilities and the quality and quantity of hospital supplies.[34] They requested no financial compensation; all would be accomplished through private donations and money raised at " fairs" held in major cities. At a Sanitary Commission fair, one could buy food, handicrafts, art objects, and similar items; most of these made by women in the relief societies. It was later claimed that the fairs held in New York and Philadelphia, alone, raised more than one million dollars each.[35]

The U.S. government, including President Lincoln, met the Sanitary Commission's proposal with skepticism. The government felt it could handle the situation and the civilian organization would only be duplicating their efforts. However, the delegation included some very influential personalities and had strong public support. On June 13, 1861, the President signed the order creating the United States Sanitary Commission. Dr. Bellows became its president. Its first executive secretary was Frederick Law Olmstead, the well-known New York architect and designer of that city's Central Park. The role that the Sanitary Commission would serve remained to be seen, and the event that would illustrate just how important these civilian relief agencies would be was not long in coming.

The first major battle between the Union and the Confederacy was fought on Sunday, July 21, 1861. The First Battle of Bull Run occurred about 30 miles from Washington, D.C. Both the North and the South expected this one battle to decide the outcome of the war and settle their differences. Perhaps they anticipated a few casualties, but no one was prepared for what was about to take place. After Fort Sumpter, Lincoln had called for 75,000 volunteer troops to enlist for 90 days; surely more than enough men and time to put down the Southern rebellion. On this hot July day, 35,000 of these men, under the command of General Irvin McDowell, would meet 20,000 Confederates under the command of General P.G.T. Beauregard. Both sides had dressed in their new, clean uniforms. Men stopped to pick berries, fill canteens, and rest and relax along the way. Hundreds of Washingtonians had come out to see the show. They arrived in their carriages, with their picnic lunches, all set for an afternoon of excitement and entertainment.

After several hours of fighting, and the arrival of reinforcements commanded by Confederate Gen. Joseph E. Johnston, the Confederates proved their superiority on the field. The Union line broke and McDowell gave the order to retreat. Unfortunately, the road back to Washington was clogged with civilians, who had decided that they had best get out of the area, also. In a short time panic set in. Soldiers overran civilians. Military wagons slammed into civilian buggies. Confederate shells burst all around. The retreat soon became bedlam.

By the end of the afternoon 2,700 Union soldiers were dead, wounded, or missing. Confederate losses totaled 1,981. Nearly 5,000 young, healthy American men were gone.

Dead and wounded soldiers lay strewn across the battlefield. Moaning and screaming for help, some of the wounded lay there for hours. Civilian ambulance drivers had been hired by the U.S. government, and in the mass panic of retreat, they had raced back to Washington, empty. Medical operations were completely unorganized. No one knew who had what authority. Field "first-aid" stations were poorly utilized. Many regimental surgeons would care only for the men of their own regiment, and leave others to suffer and die. Most injured soldiers walked or were carried back to Washington by other soldiers. In an investigation after the battle, the Sanitary Commission could not find one single instance of a wounded man having reached the capital in an ambulance.[36]

If the Sanitary Commission needed a defining moment to prove their necessity and importance, Bull Run was it. The U.S. government lost a lot of credibility that day. Its soldiers were ill-prepared, and its commanding generals proved lacking. What was supposed to be a show of force turned out to be just the opposite. The army had sent its soldiers to be slaughtered and couldn't care for them after it had. That July morning had started out with the air of a holiday and had taken on the aura of hell. The government clearly had to make some drastic changes.

As was to happen several times throughout the war, the first change made was in commanding generals. McDowell was removed, and General George B. McClellan was placed in command of the Army of the Potomac.

In one of his first dispatches to Washington, McClellan makes a plea for better medical organization and requests the input of the Sanitary Commission.

On September 13, 1861, to Simon Cameron, Secretary of War, McClellan writes:

> Proper arrangement in field and hospital for the sick and wounded of an army is one of the most imperative, and has always been found one of the most difficult duties of a government. From its very nature it should be under the immediate direction of the commanding general, and the whole organization entrusted to him, free from tedious delays, inconvenient formalities, and inefficient action incident to every bureau system, however ably administered.
> The Medical Bureau of the United States, like every other branch of the military service, was organized in reference to a very small army, operating generally in small divisions, and in time of peace, and hence it could not fail to be inadequate to the sudden and enormous exigencies of the present war, while its failure affords no ground of imputation or reproach against the distinguished medical officers entrusted with its administration. By no administrative talent can a system devised for the purposes of small divisions of an army (not exceeding in the whole 12,000 men) be adapted to the necessities of an army of 100,000, actively operating upon a great theater of war. To meet their wants, there must be a medical system commensurate with the army, and the nature of its operations so organized as to be in harmonious action with every other branch of service and under the same military command. The humane and disinterested services of the Sanitary Commission have enabled them to make several judicious suggestions, and their labors entitle them to the gratitude of the Army and of the country.
> The following suggestions by them are worthy of approval and immediate adoption:
> 1st. The appointment of a medical director of the Army of the Potomac by its commanding general, with such powers as he may deem proper from time to time to commit to such director.
> 2d. The immediate organization of an ambulance corps, to act under the medical director's command.
> 3d. The employment of an adequate corps of male and female nurses by the medical director, to act under his supervision.
> 4th. That "the relations of the Sanitary Commission and the Medical Bureau be placed on a basis of entire confidence and cooperation; that their disinterested counsel be received without jealousy."

These suggestions of the Commission merit and receive the cordial sanction of the Commanding General. He concurs with them in their judgment "that they have earned the right to the confidence of the Department which originally, with generous reliance, called them into being, and does not doubt that they still enjoy this confidence"; and he agrees with them in the wish "to see it extended fully from the Medical Bureau."[37]

The Sanitary Commission could not have hoped for a better endorsement. From that point on they seem to have become a respected and necessary part of the medical organization. Their duties included input regarding the location of camps, camp hygiene and sanitation matters, and camp inspections. They were involved in the supply of food, clothing, and medical supplies. Along with every corps rode at least one Sanitary Commission wagon, complete with items such as beef stock, chloroform, bandages, surgeon's silk, brandy and other "stimulants", writing paper, and chewing tobacco.[38]

The following is just a partial list of the supplies and goods the Sanitary Commission sent to Gettysburg after the July, 1863 battle:

Drawers, woolen	5,310 pairs
Drawers, cotton	1,833 pairs
Shirts, woolen	7,158
Shirts, cotton	3,266
Pillows	2,114
Blankets	1,007
Sheets	274
Stockings	5,818 pairs
Shoes	4,000 pairs
Combs	1500
Soap	250 pounds
Basins and cups	7,000
Bandage linen	110 barrels
Splinting/Dressing plaster	16 rolls
Crutches	1,200 pairs

In addition, the Sanitary Commission sent 60 tons of perishable items in refrigerated railroad cars. This shipment included 11,000 pounds of meat, 8,500 dozen eggs, 675 bushels of vegetables, and 12,900 loaves of bread.

The Commission also sent several wagonloads that the soldiers especially appreciated. In those were 1250 bottles of brandy, 1,168 bottles of whiskey, 1,148 bottles of wine, and 600 gallons of ale. Also included were 100 pounds of tobacco and 1,000 pipes.[39]

In light of the above Gettysburg inventory, Sanitary Commission Publication No.78, issued on January 1, 1864, should not be too surprising; its title...*An Answer to the Question-"Why does the Sanitary Commission need so much Money?"*[40]

Throughout the course of the war, the U.S. Sanitary Commission published ninety-five publications on topics of medical importance. These were distributed to medical personnel for informational and educational purposes. Most of these pamphlets contained information on the subjects of camp sanitation and personal hygiene. Some contained information on more technical medical and surgical matters. The majority were distributed early in the war. As information was disseminated, and the army adopted many of their recommendations, their publications became fewer.

Military personnel in the field, from private to general, came to rely on the intervention and supplies of the Sanitary Commission. The services they provided are illustrated by a few of the many dispatches requesting their aid:[41]

February 9, 1863
Major General C.S. Hamilton to General U.S. Grant
... referring to the subject of cotton in the hands of Captain Eddy. ... a portion of the cotton is fully liable to confiscation, and the agents of the United States Sanitary Commission have applied to me for a few bales to be made into comforters for the hospitals.

July 25, 1863
Medical Inspector Edward P. Vollum to Washington, D.C.
(arriving at Gettysburg)...found about 2,000 slightly wounded men collected at a point a mile from town, where the trains stopped, without food, shelter, or attendance for the night. Fortunately, through the agents of the Sanitary Commission, these men were all fed, and some 300 sheltered that night.

February 1864
Field Surgeon A. Majer to the Chief Medical Officer, District of Florida
Send immediately a train of cars with bales of hay, lint, bandages, and stimulants.
Call on the Sanitary Commission

Besides the publication of informative pamphlets and medical supply distribution, the Sanitary Commission was also politically active in terms of administrative reform. To a significant degree, the appointment of William Hammond, to the position of Surgeon General, was due to their endorsement.

In 1863, they began publishing a directory that included the names of the sick and wounded soldiers in every Union general hospital, in an effort to aid families in search of ill or injured loved ones. The Commission also set up a number of "lodges" where soldiers could stay on their way to camp or on their way back home.

Other important Union relief agencies included the Western Sanitary Commission, which operated in the western theater of the war, and the United States Christian Commission, which distributed books, magazines, newspapers, and Bibles. The Christian Commission also issued writing materials and postage stamps.[42]

In the South, there was no central organization to compare to the U.S. Sanitary Commission. Several Relief Societies and Women's Aid Societies provided similar functions. These groups were organized at the local or state level; often by the wives of Southern officers.

V - AUXILIARY MEDICAL PERSONNEL

Support services in the Medical Department were provided by a wide variety of groups and individuals. To provide medical care to ill and injured soldiers, Civil War surgeons required personnel to transport troops from battlefield to hospital, assistance in surgery, and help in dispensing medication, cleaning operating areas, changing bed linens, and changing wound dressings.

Brigade surgeons had the responsibility of training and drilling the regimental musicians and other men of the regiment in stretcher detail. Since there was no need for music at the time of battle, the bandsmen were trained to carry stretchers and remove injured soldiers from the battlefield. Often, their interest in battlefield medicine proved much less than their interest in music, and they disappeared shortly after the shooting began. Occasionally, several soldiers were assigned specifically to stretcher detail, in addition to the bandsmen. These might be men with minor injuries, or men who had shown that they weren't much use in actual fighting. As the war progressed, and the ambulance service became more refined and efficient, stretcher detail was often provided by men specifically trained for this purpose.

Hospital Stewards

Every surgeon had a hospital steward appointed to assist him. The hospital steward was a non-commissioned officer with the rank of sergeant. The steward's duties were fully described in, "*The Hospital Steward's Manual*", by Joseph Janvier Woodward, M.D., a leading physician of his day. This text was written at the request of Surgeon General Hammond. It received critical acclaim and endorsement by that office, and became the standard reference in terms of the responsibilities of the various classes of hospital attendants. In addition to its information regarding hospital stewards, it outlined the duties and responsibilities of ward-masters, nurses, female nurses, cooks, and laundresses.

The requirements and expectations for stewards were as follows:

> The candidate for enlistment or appointment as hospital steward should be not less than eighteen nor more than thirty-five years of age. He must be able-bodied and free from disease. Previous to his enlistment he is inspected by a medical officer, in the same manner as any other recruit, and will be rejected if found laboring under any disease or disability which would reject a recruit. He should be of honest and upright character, of temperate habits, and of good general intelligence. He must have a competent knowledge of the English language, and be able to write legibly and spell correctly. This point must be satisfactorily ascertained before he can be enlisted, as without this qualification it will be impossible for him to keep the books and records, or to attend to the general business of the hospital. In addition, he must have sufficient practical knowledge of pharmacy to enable him to take exclusive charge of the dispensary, must be practically acquainted with such points of minor surgery as the application of bandages and dressings, the extraction of teeth, and the application of cups and leeches, and must have such knowledge of cooking as will enable him to superintend efficiently this important branch of hospital service.[43]

Sections of the manual presented the specific duties of the steward. Duties varied somewhat depending on whether the surgeon, to which the steward was assigned, was working in a field hospital or a general hospital. Also, some stewards were assigned to aid the assistant surgeons manning the dressing stations on the front line. If a hospital contained greater than 150 patients, more than one steward would be appointed. Each steward was assigned specific hospital duties, delegated by the surgeon in charge. Under the direction of the surgeon, the steward was responsible for the general supervision of the hospital. His responsibilities included the supervision and discipline of the other hospital attendants, ventilation and lighting of the hospital, purchasing and caring for hospital supplies, and supervision of food services. Other important duties included the maintenance of the hospital dispensary (pharmacy), and the preparation and administration of prescribed medications. He also assisted the surgeon in performing dressing changes, minor surgery, and other procedures. Woodward's manual provided great detail in regards to the functions of the steward; from specific instructions on food preparation (including recipes), to proper hospital ventilation, lighting and heating. There were sections concerning the construction of latrines, and bathing and laundry facilities. In terms of technical skills, sections were devoted to the application of bandages and dressings and other required procedures. These procedures, for which the hospital steward would be responsible, included "cupping", the application of leeches, extraction of teeth, and "injections".

Cupping consisted of the application of glass or metal cups to the patient's skin surface. Cups were placed on various areas of the body. For example, they were applied to the chest to treat pneumonia, or to the abdomen to treat gastroenteritis or peritonitis. Air would be extracted from the cup to produce a vacuum. The manner in which the air was removed depended on the exact apparatus being used. Many utilized a small air pump, connected by a hose, to the apex of the cup. Some cups were simply heated and applied to the skin. As the air inside cooled (and therefore contracted) a vacuum was produced. "Dry cupping" involved the placement of cups on intact skin. These would be left in place until swelling, erythema, and bruising developed. "Wet cupping" involved the placement of cups on skin that had been previously incised, either by a lancet or scarificator. A scarificator was a spring-loaded, mechanical device that produced multiple (usually 12 to 16) superficial skin incisions. The "wet cup" would be left in place until an ounce or so of blood had pooled into the cup.

Cupping was originally performed to rid the body of "bad humors" or "bad blood", factors which were felt to be responsible for many diseases. By the time of the Civil War, an alternative theory was developing, that the cups were pulling disease-producing internal inflammation or "excitation" to the surface, where it could dissipate.

Wet cupping was actually a form of local blood-letting, and leeches were often used to perform the same function. Two kinds of leeches were employed. The smaller American leech was reported to draw off an estimated sixth to an eighth of an ounce of blood, each. The much larger European leech reportedly could draw as much as two to three ounces. Woodward describes:

> Leeches may be kept on hand in good condition, for a long time, in
> tubs filled with water, at the bottom of which turf or peat is placed.
> The water should be changed about once a week. After they have been

used, some means should be employed to evacuate the blood they have
gorged: otherwise, they generally die. This may be done sprinkling
them with salt, or pouring salt water upon them, which causes them to
eject the contents of their stomachs. A better plan, perhaps, is to make
two small punctures on the back of the leech...through these the blood
escapes, and the little wound subsequently heals.[44]

Throughout the war, both sides persisted in the use of local measures such as cupping, leeching, or even irritation of the skin with chemical compounds, in an effort to draw out inflammation. With experience, and lack of any recognizable benefits, these techniques were gradually used less frequently. In fact, by the end of the war, the Sanitary Commission approved the use of leeches only when applied to the scalp as a treatment for severe headache.

Systemic blood-letting, by which large volumes of blood were drained by venesection (opening a vein with a lancet or scalpel), was already falling out of favor in civilian practice by the time of the Civil War. It did not take long for surgeons to note that their patients, many of whom had lost large volumes of blood, or were seriously dehydrated, only worsened or even died as a result of systemic blood-letting. Before long, the practice of systemic blood-letting was generally abandoned. Both the Union and Confederate Medical Departments condemned the practice early in the war.

The "injections" the stewards would be responsible for were actually enemas. Rectal enemas were used to treat constipation. Occasionally, various medications would be instilled rectally. Medication injections into the urethra were used in the treatment of gonorrhea.

Obviously, the hospital steward had many significant responsibilities. As in every other branch of medical service, some performed better than others. Many of these men were pharmacists or medical students before the war, and had already been instilled with some valuable knowledge and experience. The steward's pay was $22.00 a month.

Hospital stewards were also used by the Confederate Medical Department and performed essentially the same functions as their northern counterparts. They also held the rank of sergeant. Appointees were "to be skilled in pharmacy and to possess such qualities as honesty, reliability, intelligence, and temperance...the steward was to be responsible for the cleanliness of the wards and kitchens, patients and attendants, and all articles in use."[45]

Nurses
Nursing duties, in field hospitals located near battle sites, were usually provided by convalescing soldiers or the above-mentioned musicians. Therefore, the majority of nurses in field hospitals were men. Occasionally, a soldier would be cared for, in a field hospital, by members of his own family, if the hospital was located close to his home. Almost every major engagement attracted local women who wanted to help administer medical care near the battlefield, but this was generally discouraged.

23

Female nurses were usually employed in general hospitals, located in cities remote from the actual fighting, although there were exceptions. Florence Nightingale, famous for her role as the supervisor of nursing in British Army hospitals during the Crimean War, had already illustrated the important role female nurses could serve in military hospitals. In America, prior to the Civil War, ill or injured patients were nursed in their own homes by family members, or in hospitals, which primarily served the destitute, and were staffed by nuns from various Catholic orders. During wartime, the tremendous number of casualties made such staffing insufficient.

In 1861, Dorthea Dix was already well-known as the founder of specialized institutions for the mentally insane. She was acquainted with the work of the British Sanitary Commission during the Crimean War, and had visited the hospitals reformed by Florence Nightingale on the Black Sea.[46] On April 19, 1861, seven days after the firing on Fort Sumpter, Dix offered her services to the Secretary of War, to provide trained, lay nurses to staff military hospitals. In June, she became the "Superintendent of Female Nurses."

The prospect of young females taking care of young men concerned the conservative faction of society. There was some degree of public outcry at such a "radical" idea. However, the plan was generally well-received. Miss Dix was a woman that commanded respect and the plan had the support of the Sanitary Commission.

Dix sent out the word and literally thousands of women submitted their applications. In keeping with the Victorian principles of the day, each candidate had to be, "past thirty years of age, healthy, plain almost to repulsion in dress, and devoid of personal attractions." They had to know "how to cook all kinds of low diet" and avoid "colored dresses, hoops, curls, jewelry, and flowers on their bonnets." They must "look neat themselves, and keep their boys and wards the same. Must write and read for the boys, but not from any book or newspaper; must be in their own rooms at taps, or nine o'clock, unless obliged to be with the sick; must not go to any place of amusement in the evening; must not walk out with any patient or officer except on business; must be willing to take the forty cents per day that is allowed by the government, to assist in supplying what the rations will not furnish in food."[47]

J.J. Woodward, in "*The Hospital Steward's Manual*" provides exhausting detail of the duties expected of the hospital nurses; "the chief nurse will see that the beds are duly made up in the morning...chamberpots, bedpans, and urinals are emptied...that the ward is properly swept and cleaned daily...that meals are furnished...that medications are sent for when notification of their readiness is received from the dispensary and that they are administered to the patient...that the ward is properly ventilated and free from all close or unpleasant odors...that the ward is properly lighted at night and warmed in the winter."[48] Nurses were also responsible for bathing the patients, and checking for scabies and body lice.

Unfortunately, not all went smoothly. Miss Dix was somewhat lacking in administrative talents, and she did not always get along with medical officers. In a political world, she was not very political. She demanded special rights and duties for her nurses. In a male-dominated medical system, she ran into nothing but obstacles. Initially, she insisted that only her personally screened and approved nurses could work in the hospitals. However, after making enemies of certain high ranking medical staff, including Acting Surgeon

General Joseph K. Barnes, other nurses were granted "special appointments." These included women who could not meet Dix's strict standards or mesh with her personality.

Prior to the Civil War, nursing, as a profession, did not exist in the United States. There were no nursing schools; these women would have to receive on-the-job training.

Due to lack of standardization, there was tremendous variety in the women who would assume the role of Civil War nurse. They ranged from poorly schooled or illiterate young girls to well-educated matronly socialites. Several were the wives of soldiers.

Although many assumed an important role and found their "niche" in the care of the patient, many were disdained by the surgeons they worked with. It has been said that their greatest failing was self-righteousness. They came on the scene with their own agenda, and it wasn't well-received. They were outspoken critics of smoking, drinking, and swearing; veritable staples of military life. They often ignored prescriptions for medications and diet, instead substituting home remedies or other medications as they deemed fit.

However, many were to work within the existing medical system, and provide a useful, respected and appreciated service. Patients preferred the women nurses who approached their care in a kinder, gentler fashion. They became mother and sister substitutes for these homesick men, confined to a hospital bed, far from home.

Compared to their lay counterparts, nuns, as nurses, were held in high regard by the surgeons. From pre-war days, many had experience in dealing with hospitalized patients. At the outset of the war, they were the only women with anything even resembling nursing experience. Their duties in schools, orphanages, hospitals, and pest houses included caring for ill residents and patients. From this previous exposure, many had developed immunity to a variety of childhood illnesses; another factor that would become important as they cared for ill Civil War soldiers; an advantage many lay nurses did not possess. Also, their training stressed obedience, which probably was beneficial in dealing with the personalities of the medical officers they would be working with. Orders that supplied nurses included the Daughters of Charity, Sisters of Mercy, Sisters of Saint Joseph, and the Sisters of the Holy Cross.[49]

For the Union, approximately 3,200 women would serve as nurses. The number of women who served as nurses for the Confederacy is unknown.

The South had no equivalent personality to that of Dorthea Dix, and the Confederacy never developed a formal nursing program. However, many women did volunteer for nursing duty on their own initiative. Convalescing soldiers were also utilized as nurses. As in the North, Catholic sisters provided valued nursing services. Due to the lack of a civilian nursing program, the South used relatively more nuns as nurses than did the North.

It should be emphasized, that nuns remained completely non-partisan throughout the war. They worked as "volunteers" and received no compensation from either government. As the war front shifted back and forth, nuns stayed on at the same hospitals, alternately caring for Union and Confederate soldiers. Catholic sisters were allowed to pass through the lines without question. The distinctive habits they wore served as their sole identification and authorization to move about freely. It was stated, "Their religious habit was their certificate of honor and of service, and by order of those in authority in the two armies, no countersign was ever demanded." For all the times that these nuns passed through the lines, there is no recorded instance of a sister betraying this trust.[50]

A nurse that requires special mention is Clara Barton. Nicknamed "The Angel of the Battlefield," she was one of the nurses who actually served on the battlefield as well as in field hospitals. At the outset of the war, she was a clerk in the U.S. Patent Office in Washington, D.C. She soon organized an agency to obtain and distribute medical supplies. She was critical of the way medical matters were being managed by the government, and was quite vocal in her opinions. Even though she performed some nursing-type duties, her basic function was, in fact, similar to that of an independent relief agency. She went from battlefield to battlefield hauling a wagon stocked with her own supplies. She worked strictly on a volunteer basis and never received any monetary compensation for her efforts. After the Civil War, she went to Europe for a rest. During the Franco-Prussian War (1870-1871), she became involved with the International Red Cross. In 1881, she started the American Red Cross and served as its president until 1904.

One of Clara Barton's major accomplishments was her role in encouraging the U.S. Government to sign the medical neutrality agreements at the initial Geneva Convention in August, 1864.

The cause of ensuring neutrality for medical personnel during wartime was initially taken up by General Stonewall Jackson after the Battle of Winchester, in May, 1862. Jackson took the position that, "as surgeons did not make war, they should not suffer its penalties." The neutral status of surgeons was formally agreed to by Generals McClellan and Lee.[51] Subsequently, the Adjutant General's Office in Washington issued General Orders No. 60, dated June 6, 1862, which stated, "...the principle being recognized that [Confederate] medical officers so held by the United States shall be immediately and unconditionally discharged." In response, the Confederate Adjutant and Inspector General's Office published General Orders No. 45, on June 26, 1862, which directed, "the immediate and unconditional discharge of all [Union] medical officers held in Southern prisons."[52]

At the first Geneva Convention, in 1864, with the encouragement and endorsement of Clara Barton, these concepts were signed into international law, when representatives of sixteen countries pledged to respect the neutrality of civilians, medical personnel, and hospital ships bearing the emblem of the Red Cross.

PART 2

<u>ON THE BATTLEFIELD</u>:

Transportation of the
Wounded
and
The Hospital System

I - THE BATTLEFIELD

Civil War soldier, Lucius Barber, describes a battle scene in his memoirs:

> No one can adequately describe the terrific fighting during the day.
> The enemy... would mass their strength against the weakest portion
> of our line, and then with demoniacal yells would hurl themselves
> against it, and for a time the shock of arms would make the earth
> tremble. Giant trees would writhe and twist before the iron hail and
> come crashing to the ground. The screeching shells, rending
> everything before them, cutting huge limbs from the trees, striking the
> earth and throwing up clouds of dirt, formed a scene of terrific
> grandeur. ...It seems as though the very earth was opening up to
> swallow up the combatants. The air was black with fine shot and shell.
> For an hour this storm of iron hail would rage.[53]

In his report to Confederate Army Headquarters, Major General Thomas C. Hindman describes the scene at Fayetteville, Arkansas, during the Battle of Prarie Grove in December, 1862:

> There was no place of shelter upon any portion of the field. Wounds
> were given and deaths inflicted by the enemy's artillery in the ranks of
> the reserves as well as in the front rank. During five hours, shell, solid
> shot, grape and canister, and storms of bullets swept the entire ground.
> Many gallant officers, and many soldiers equally brave, fell dead or
> wounded, but their comrades stood as firm as iron.[54]

The aftermath of a Civil War battle is something that is difficult to imagine. A Civil War reenactment, no matter how large and historically accurate, cannot adequately represent the overwhelming devastation and carnage . The special effects of film, no matter how detailed and gruesome, cannot give one the true sense of being in the midst of it all. The sounds, the sights, the smells, and the horrific pain and anguish; none can be experienced or comprehended on a truly visceral level. Undoubtedly, that is best.

The American continent has never seen pain and death in such magnitude. More Americans died in the Civil War than in all other wars in which they have fought, to date, combined. Casualty numbers are almost unfathomable.

Shiloh, Tennessee   April 6-7, 1862; 24,000 casualties. In this one battle, the total number of casualties easily surpassed the American casualties in the Revolutionary War, the War of 1812, and the Mexican War, combined.

Antietam, Maryland   September 17, 1862; 25,000 casualties. The single bloodiest day in American history. A record that still stands.

Gettysburg, Pennsylvania   July 1-3,1863; 51,000 casualties. Confederate casualties of 28,000 represented over thirty-five percent of Lee's Army of Northern Virginia.

<u>Wilderness, Virginia</u>   May 5-7, 1864; 17,666 Union casualties. Thousands of wounded men died when the woods caught fire after the battle. Soldiers listened to their dying screams for hours.

John Casler, a Confederate soldier, describes:

> "...On the left side of our line...the scene beggars description. The dead and badly wounded from both sides were laying where they fell. The woods, taking fire that night from the shells, burnt rapidly and roasted the wounded men alive. As we went to bury them we could see where they had tried to keep the fire from them by scratching the leaves away as far as they could reach. But it availed not; they were burned to a crisp."[55]

<u>Cold Harbor, Virginia</u>   June 3, 1864; In a devastating frontal assault, Grant lost over 12,000 men. 7,000 of them fell in the first seven minutes.

This list could go on. The Civil War involved over 50 major battles, 5,000 minor engagements, and thousands more small skirmishes. Each exchange of gunfire resulted in injury and death. These grim totals give an impression of the magnitude of devastation, on human life, that the Civil War would wreak. However, no matter how large or small the battle, how many or how few the total number of casualties, to the individual soldier it made no difference. To the individual wounded soldier, the pain was all his; his own personal hell. A family's world collapsed at the report of a single death or serious injury. Magnify that individual suffering by hundreds of thousands, and the magnitude of the anguish caused by the Civil War begins to become appreciated.

A Civil War battlefield presented an unimaginably gruesome image. Over 94% of battle wounds were caused by gunshot. The vast majority were inflicted by the minie ball. Artillery shells, canister, and grapeshot each took their toll, estimated at 6% of casualties. Canister and grapeshot were loaded into cannons, the cannons leveled, and then fired into massed groups of onrushing infantry. It was like walking into the blast of a giant shotgun. Less than 1% of wounds were caused by saber or bayonet.

Battlefields were strewn with dead and dying soldiers. Men wounded in all degrees were moaning, screaming, crawling, or walking for help. Many were too wounded to moan or move at all. Bodies were missing arms, legs, and heads. Disemboweled soldiers lay dead or horribly suffering. There were many reports of whole groups of soldiers charging up to a cannon barrel, just as it discharged its load of canister or grapeshot; essentially being blasted into unidentifiable pieces.

Of the men who died of battle-related injuries, approximately two-thirds died on the battlefield. One-third died later, in field or general hospitals.

II - BATTLEFIELD TRANSPORT AND HOSPITAL FACILITIES

During the course of an engagement, casualties began to accumulate by the hundreds and thousands. The first step in the treatment of the wounded was getting them transported to medical facilities. The second step was to have competent medical facilities available.

As previously noted, medical transportation after the Battle of Bull Run, in July, 1861, was essentially non-existent. Civilians had been hired as ambulance wagon drivers, and in their fear, hurried back to Washington as the fighting grew intense. In their exodus, they brought no casualties from the field. Wounded soldiers made their way to hospitals by any means they could.

The Medical Director of the Army of the Potomac, at the time of the battle, was Surgeon W.S. King. After the battle, he rode around the battlefield accompanied by General McDowell trying to make some sense of the chaos. Field hospitals were poorly located. Regimental surgeons would only care for the wounded from their own regiments. Soldiers wandered the field looking for help. Many eventually made it on their own to Washington, thirty miles away, and were treated in the general hospitals there. In desperation, Surgeon King finally got off his wagon and began assisting the field surgeons himself. It was clear that an effective system of medical transportation and treatment would have to be developed, literally, from the ground up.

At the outset of the war, medical care was organized and provided solely at the regimental level. As we have seen, each regiment had a surgeon, an assistant surgeon, and a hospital steward. The bandsmen and a few other men were assigned to transport the wounded, from where they lay on the battlefield, to the location of the regimental medical staff. The wounded were usually picked up on hand-litters or stretchers. During the course of the war, the U.S. Army issued over 50,000 hand-litters for transportation of the wounded. Occasionally, stretchers were improvised by passing poles or muskets through the sleeves of coats. Gates, window shutters, ladders, boards and blankets, and anything else that would carry an injured man between two stretcher bearers were also used.[56] Wounded, who were able to walk, were expected to make their own way to the surgeons.

Figure 1: Standard Military Issue Hand Litter

The wounded walked, or were carried, to the regiment's "primary" or "dressing" station. The dressing station was set up on the battlefield just out of gun range. Due to the waxing and waning nature of the location of the front line, this first-aid station was often moved several times during the course of the battle. The dressing station was manned by the regiment's assistant surgeon and a steward or orderly.

As the wounded arrived at the dressing station, they were quickly assessed. Whiskey was given to counteract shock. Basins of water and sponges were used to clean wounds for rapid inspection. Minor wounds were dressed with linen bandages, and, if capable, the wounded soldier was sent back into battle. Pressure dressings were applied to large lacerations in order to control bleeding. In cases of uncontrollable arterial hemorrhaging, tourniquets were applied. Many of these tourniquets were left in place until the patient was transferred from the battlefield to a field hospital. Some tourniquets were left in place for several hours, cutting off all blood flow to the extremity, therefore contributing to the loss of limbs. Splints were applied to extremities in cases of obvious fracture. After a soldier was stabilized at the dressing station, he was placed in an ambulance for transport to a field hospital.

Early in the war, field hospitals were staffed and supplied at the regimental level. Buildings near the battlefield, but out of the range of cannon fire, were procured by regimental surgeons for use as field hospitals. To be safely out of range, these buildings were usually located a mile and a half to two miles from the battle. These buildings included private homes, barns, sheds, and other outbuildings, as well as churches and other public structures. Union field hospitals were often identified by a white flag with a large yellow "H" in the center. Most of the furniture was removed, and doors were often taken off their hinges for use as operating tables. Most surgical procedures, including amputations, were performed in the field hospital. Soldiers were then transferred to a general hospital for recuperation. General hospitals were usually located in large cities, distant from the fighting.

After the debacle at Bull Run, the ambulance service and field hospital facilities began a steady improvement which continued throughout the war. Shortly after that battle, Surgeon King was replaced as Medical Director of the Army of the Potomac, by Dr. Charles Tripler. Tripler assumed that position on August 12, 1861, and immediately began to make changes. Tripler made changes that would affect the delivery of medical care on the battlefield, as well as in field and general hospitals.

In February, 1862, after the Battle of Fort Donelson, in the West, Surgeon H.S. Hewitt, the medical director of Grant's army, organized twenty-eight regimental medical staffs into four divisional field hospitals. He organized the regimental ambulances by brigade into large ambulance trains that could be used wherever needed; without regard to their particular regiments. Two months later, at Shiloh, Surgeon B.J.D. Irwin, of the Army of the Ohio, converted a number of tents into a large unified field hospital; the first of its kind in the war. By April, 1862, the western army had reached the stage of a brigade level ambulance corps and brigade level field hospitals. This allowed for efficient distribution of supplies and staff. Surgery was performed only by surgeons who had demonstrated surgical skill. This system would remain, in the West, with minor changes, for virtually the remainder of the war.[57]

Unfortunately, Tripler, in the East, was still clinging to the regimental system. He seemed reluctant to alter the existing system, even though he recognized its shortcomings. To his credit, he provided for three hospital tents (instead of one) for each regiment in the Army of the Potomac. He improved the general hospitals in Washington, D.C. and Alexandria, Virginia. He initiated an effort to clean up the army's base camps. In April, he moved the main army camp, from the damp flats near Arlington, to a better location. A third of the men in that camp had been seriously ill with malaria, dysentery, or typhoid. By February, the new campsite contained only nine significantly ill soldiers, out 10,000 men in camp.[58]

Tripler encouraged better reporting from the regimental surgeons, and the removal of incompetent medical staff. Fortunately, some of the surgeons in his staff took it upon themselves to organize their personnel and equipment into brigade level facilities.

Tripler also noted deficiencies in ambulance transportation. He partly acknowledged that an ambulance corps might have some advantages, but "regulations and other obstacles effectually prevented any notable advance in that direction."[59]

To his credit, Tripler was cognizant of the fact that the Army's standard two-wheeled ambulance was terribly engineered for it s purpose. They were uncomfortable, too small, and tipped easily. As a result, they were nicknamed "avalanches" by the medical staff and soldiers. Several medical men, including Tripler himself, developed much improved four-wheeled designs. In January, 1862, the Army of the Potomac had 314 two-wheeled ambulances and only 71 of the four-wheeled design. By the beginning of the Peninsular Campaign, in April, 1862, the Army had 177 of the four-wheeled type. Before the war was half over, the two-wheeled variety was essentially obsolete, and general orders provided that only four-wheeled ambulances be used.[60]

Figure 2: Two-Wheeled Ambulance

Several civilians, as well as military medical personnel, pushed for the organization of a large-scale, unified ambulance corps, but Tripler remained steadfast in his insistence on adhering to current rules and regulations. His blind endorsement of the antiquated regimental system is hard to understand.

About this time, the U.S. Sanitary Commission was pushing it's agenda of medical and political reform. With their backing, Surgeon General Hammond was appointed in April, 1862. Sanitary Commission inspectors began conducting detailed evaluations of all aspects regarding the provision of medical care and the condition of medical facilities. Their reports soon began arriving in Washington. It was apparent to the inspectors and the Medical Department that Tripler was not performing to their expectations.

On July 4, 1862, Surgeon Tripler was replaced by Dr. Jonathan Letterman, as Medical Director of the Army of the Potomac. Later that month, a law was enacted which provided for the designation of a brigade surgeon to supervise the regimental surgeons and oversee all medical care in his brigade. Each army already had a medical director to whom the brigade surgeons would now report. This chain of command resulted in accountability, which improved the delivery of medical care, and helped disseminate information and reform measures.

Immediately upon his appointment, Letterman requested two hundred ambulances and one thousand hospital tents. By August 2, he had already submitted to General McClellan a plan for the development of an ambulance corps. Under his plan, all ambulances were taken away from individual regiments and placed under division control. The total number of ambulances issued depended on the number and size of the regiments in the division. This number came out to about one ambulance for every one-hundred and fifty men. The ambulances of each division were kept in a train. Occasionally, these divisional trains were combined into corps trains. Ambulance drivers would be hired and trained by the Medical Department, rather than the Quartermaster Corps, which continued to hire unreliable civilian drivers. In March, 1863, Grant approved this system for use by his Army of the Tennessee, the only significant change in the western army's medical organization since April, 1862.[61]

In the East, the first test of this new system was at Antietam, on September 17, 1862. This bloodiest day in American history produced 10,000 wounded Union soldiers. All were removed from the battlefield within 24 hours. By comparison, after the Second Battle of Bull Run, August 29-30, 1862, which occurred just prior to the institution of Letterman's policies, 3,000 wounded men still lay on the battlefield three days after the fighting had stopped. Some lay on the field up to seven days without food or medical attention. Many of those reported as "killed in action", no doubt died a long, slow, and lingering death.[62]

The treatment of the wounded from Antietam was to be the birth of efficient and effective medical care in the East. The ambulance drivers were soldiers selected and trained by the Medical Department. Over 300 four-wheeled ambulances were made available just before the battle. Letterman did not have time to designate specific division level field hospitals, but regimental hospitals were ordered to merge into divisional units "so far as practicable."[63] In anticipation of this major engagement, Letterman had arranged for extra medical supplies to be sent from Washington, Alexandria, and Baltimore. With these supplies, along with those sent by the Sanitary Commission, U.S. surgeons could adequately care for the 10,000 wounded Union soldiers, as well as 4,000 Confederate wounded that lay behind Union lines. In short order, the wounded were evacuated to general hospitals in Frederick, Maryland. These also had been selected, staffed, and equipped by Letterman, prior to the outbreak of the battle. The ambulances moved on fixed schedules between the field hospitals and Frederick, stopping at Middletown, halfway to their destination, where an army relief station gave food, drink, and any necessary medical attention to the wounded.[64]

Figure 3: Four-Wheeled Ambulance

Letterman's structure for the ambulance corps would eventually be adopted by the U.S. Government for use in all its armies. The Ambulance Corps Act was signed into law on March 11, 1864. This Act was pushed through Congress with the help of several civilian reformers, including a very vocal Dr. Henry I. Bowditch of Boston, whose son had died of an abdominal wound after being carried off a battlefield draped over a horse. He was the author of a pamphlet entitled, "A Brief Plea for an Ambulance System", which was widely circulated.[65]

With the same enthusiasm and efficiency that resulted in a highly effective ambulance program, Letterman attacked the problems inherent in the existing field hospital system.

When field hospitals were being staffed and supplied at the regimental level, results were generally poor. Some hospitals, caring for regiments that experienced heavy fighting, quickly became overwhelmed and ran out of supplies. Other hospitals accumulated a surplus of supplies, and most seemed unwilling to share. On October 30, 1862, Letterman adopted the system of division level field hospitals and division level medical supply. A typical division hospital train consisted of fourteen army wagons and four medical wagons, their contents being twenty-two hospital tents and the medical supplies and surgical equipment which would ordinarily be sufficient for the care of the 7,000 to 8,000 men in the division.

Under this new plan, one assistant surgeon from each regiment in the division operated a dressing station at the front; the remainder of the division's medical staff gathered at the division hospital. As before, most of these hospitals utilized pre-existing buildings near the front, although increasingly, large tent field hospitals were erected. Rather than having every regimental surgeon perform surgery, a system involving a division of labor was developed. In each division, one surgeon was designated as the Surgeon-in-Charge. Under his authority, a medical officer was assigned to keep records; another supervised the supply and distribution of food, clothing, shelter, and bedding; others functioned as wound dressers, or performed other necessary duties. Three surgeons and three assistant surgeons were assigned, specifically, to surgical duty. One of the assistants would be selected to administer anesthetics. In his "Field Hospital Order," dated October 30, 1862, Letterman mandated that, "these officers will be selected from the Division without regard to rank, but solely on account of their known prudence, judgment, and skill....be especially careful in the selection of these officers, choosing only those who have distinguished themselves for surgical skill, sound judgment, and conscientious regard for the highest interest of the wounded. In all doubtful cases, they will consult together, and a majority of them shall decide on the expediency and character of the operation."[66] As a result, only about one surgeon in fifteen was a member of the surgical team that actually performed operations. This specialization in surgical care proved to be a major advance in military medicine.[67]

Additional medical officers, hospital stewards, and any divisional nurses would also come under the superintendence of the Surgeon-in-Charge.

The Battle of Fredericksburg, Virginia, fought December 13, 1862, was the first battle that utilized the combination of Letterman's ambulance plan and field hospital system. After the battle, Dr. D.W. Brink, a Sanitary Commission inspector reported:

> ... Before closing this report I would again refer to the Medical Department of the Army. The most marked improvement is observable in all that pertains to the management of the wounded. Instead of churches, dwellings, barns and sheds, being crowded, and many remaining unsheltered, as was the case at Antietam and elsewhere after great battles, ample accommodations were provided in tents, with blankets and all essential stores. The ambulance corps is so improved that it will, I believe, compare favorably even with that of France. But above all, the organization of the Medical Corps for field and hospital service is deserving of the highest encomiums."[68]

Medical Director Jonathan Letterman had designed an effective and successful system of battlefield transportation and medical care.

After their initial treatment and/or surgery, the wounded were removed from the field hospitals by wagon or ambulance, and usually transported to a railroad depot or steamship landing. From there, they were taken by train or ship to one of the large, general hospitals for recuperation. General hospitals were military hospitals that would accept ill or injured soldiers from any military unit or post. The particular regiment, division, or corps to which the soldier belonged was irrelevant. Early in the war, most of these hospitals were set up in large, public buildings such as schools, churches, factories, or warehouses. Later, specific, specialized buildings were constructed for use as hospitals.

In both the North and the South, most general hospitals were built under the "pavilion plan." Confederate Surgeon General Samuel Preston Moore is often given credit for developing this style of hospital design, but the accuracy of this claim is unknown. In 1861, just after the Battle of Bull Run, Surgeon Moore wrote, "...the plan was adopted of erecting buildings, each one to be a ward and separate...calculated for thirty-two beds, with streets running each way, say thirty feet wide. From fifteen to twenty of such wards constituted a division, three or more divisions making a general hospital."[69] Five of these hospitals were erected outside of Richmond in 1861. With minor alterations in size, total capacity, bed arrangement, and ventilation aspects, this was the plan used by both sides, for general hospital construction, for the duration of the war.

Pavilion hospitals were divided into individual wards. Often separate units were connected to a central building by corridors, like the spokes of a wheel radiating from a central hub. In the "central hub" were located the laundry and linen storage, kitchen and food storage, and other common services. Patients in the wards were separated by types of illness or injury, allowing for specialized care. Also, if a particular illness broke out in a ward, it could be sealed off from other areas. This ward design, with the segregation of patients based on their types of medical problems, is still used in hospitals today.

Surgeon General William Hammond supervised the building of general hospitals for the Union. At the outbreak of war, in 1861, there was not one general military hospital in the United States. By 1863, there were more than 151 Union hospitals; by the war's end, there were 204, with a total bed capacity of 136,894. Washington had more than 16 general hospitals; others were located in Philadelphia; New York; Baltimore; Chattanooga; Louisville; Memphis; Nashville; City Point, Virginia; Jefferson, Indiana, and several other cities.[70]

Quincy, Illinois, the home of Dr. Samuel Everett (see Prologue), had five general hospitals. These filled to capacity in April, 1862, as wounded soldiers were carried by steamship, up the Mississippi River, after the Battle of Shiloh, in Tennessee.

In the Confederacy, the organization of the ambulance corps, field hospitals, and general hospitals developed along similar lines to the corresponding entities in the North.

Each army had a medical director who reported to the Surgeon General. Influential medical directors included Surgeon Samuel H. Stout of the Army of the Tennessee and Surgeon Lafayette Guild of the Army of Northern Virginia. Both made great strides in the improvement of battlefield transportation, field hospitals, and construction of general hospitals. Each army corps also had its own medical director. Immediately below the medical directors, in the chain of command, came the chief surgeons of the army divisions; these were appointed upon the recommendation of the medical director and were free from all regimental duties. Under a divisional chief surgeon, each brigade had a senior surgeon to oversee the brigade's overall medical performance. Individual regiments generally had one surgeon and one assistant surgeon.

Under Medical Director Guild, medical supply and services would be provided at the brigade level. However, brigade medical personnel and supplies were sometimes consolidated for the purpose of setting up divisional hospitals. In 1861, due to a lack of tents, General Lee requested division commanders to establish their field hospitals in buildings. However, Surgeon General Moore and other high-ranking officers preferred the open ventilation of tents, so a number of tent field hospitals were erected as well.

At the time of battle, an infirmary corps of about thirty men was designated, under the direction of the regimental assistant surgeon, to be responsible for the care of the wounded on the field, and for the removal from the field of those unable to walk. The infirmary corps were "usually those least effective under arms."[71] The assistant surgeon was to equip himself with, "a pocket case of instruments, ligatures, needles, pins, chloroform, morphine, alcoholic stimulants, tourniquets, bandages, lint, and splints."[72] Each pair of men from the infirmary corps was equipped with one litter, a canteen and cup, several tourniquets, four splints and some basic dressing supplies. They also carried a pint of whiskey to use as a stimulant. The assistant surgeon, along with the infirmary corps, would set up a first-aid station near the front line. This station would perform the same function as the Union's dressing station. Bleeding would be controlled, bandages, tourniquets, and splints applied. Minor wounds and injuries were treated, and soldiers who were able, could return to the battle. Transportation was arranged for removal of the seriously wounded to a field hospital.

Surgeons remained at the brigade or division field hospital and tended to those brought in by litter or ambulance. They performed the necessary surgical operations and directed the movement of the wounded to the general hospitals. As in the North, amputations and other surgical operations were to be performed at the field hospital with the least possible delay. Ambulances, and any other means of wagon transportation, were used to transport the wounded to railroad depots, steamer landings, or sometimes the entire distance to a general hospital facility. This movement was often handicapped by the lack of a sufficient number of ambulances and animals to draw them, "two of the truly serious shortages experienced by medical officers of the Southern Confederacy."[73] For the duration of the war, the South could never provide an adequate amount of ambulance transportation. Like Letterman, Guild had great hopes and expectations in terms of developing an effective and efficient ambulance corps; lack of equipment prevented this from ever becoming a reality in the South.

General hospitals were constructed throughout the war. The Southern capital of Richmond became the chief medical center of the Confederacy. Altogether, there were twenty Confederate hospitals constructed in and around Richmond. The largest of these was Chimborazo Hospital, which was the largest military hospital of the war; on either side.

The site for Chimborazo was selected by Surgeon General Moore and Dr. James B. McGaw of Richmond. On Chimborazo Hill, outside of Richmond, the Confederacy constructed the hospital, which would contain over 8,000 beds. It contained 150 wards, each one 100 feet long and 30 feet wide. Each ward housed 40 to 60 patients. The buildings were separated by alleys and streets, and, "the hospital presented the appearance of a town of considerable size." It contained five soup houses, five icehouses, Russian bathhouses, a bakery capable of making ten thousand loaves of bread daily, and a brewery in which four hundred kegs of beer were brewed at a time. A large farm, "Tree Hill", owned by Franklin Stearns, was used by the hospital for the pasturage of some two hundred cows and from three hundred to five hundred goats.[74] The hospital opened its doors on October 11, 1861. During the course of the war, approximately 76,000 patients were treated at Chimborazo.

Virginia would contain the largest number of southern hospitals, but general hospitals were located in several southern cities in the south and west. Outside of Virginia, the greatest concentration of general hospitals was to be found in Georgia. Atlanta would become a major medical center as would Montgomery, Alabama. Other cities that contained hospitals included Nashville; Chattanooga; Bowling Green, Kentucky; and Raleigh, North Carolina. By the end of the war, the Confederacy had about 150 general hospitals.

Two acts of legislation were passed by the Confederate government that did not have direct counterparts in the North.

The "Act to Provide for the Sick and Wounded of the Army in Hospitals" was passed in September, 1862. This law provided for the allotment to each hospital, of two matrons, two assistant matrons, two matrons for each ward, such other nurses and cooks as might be needed, and a ward master for each ward, "giving preference in all cases to females where their services may best subserve the purpose."[75] It was generally felt that women made better nurses than men. A formal nursing program was never adopted to compare to that of Dorthea Dix's in the North, but many women did take nursing positions in southern hospitals. They usually had no nursing training. As in the North, and to an even greater degree, the majority of skilled nursing was provided by Catholic sisters.

Another component of the Act of 1862 was an attempt to hospitalize soldiers from the same state in the same institution. Representative James Farrow of South Carolina stated that "most of the hardships which beset the soldier whilst in hospitals, grew out of the practice of mixing up soldiers from all portions of the Confederacy, in the same hospital, and scattering men from the same neighborhood and regiment." The bill provided that hospitals "be known and numbered as hospitals of a particular state" and directed that, when feasible, the sick and wounded be assigned to hospitals representing their states.[76] The divisions of Chimborazo Hospital were arranged by states. Soldiers in each division were cared for by surgeons and attendants from their state. This arrangement was felt to boost morale, improve care, and speed the healing process. Though not always achievable, it was practiced in the South as much as possible.

Another measure enacted to improve medical care became law in May, 1863. This bill directed the Surgeon General to establish a number of "way hospitals." These were to be located along the routes of important railroads, and were to furnish rations and quarters to sick or wounded furloughed or discharged soldiers, on their way home. Seventeen such hospitals were established in Virginia and North Carolina alone.[77]

As opposed to the North, the South would always have problems in obtaining hospital and medical supplies in sufficient quantities to provide decent medical care. Prior to the war, most medical supply manufacturers and their stores were located in the North. As some of these stores were captured, they were utilized by Confederate medical personnel. The vast majority of medical and surgical supplies were purchased abroad and brought in as contraband through the Union blockade. Whether treating soldiers on the battlefield or in a hospital, southern surgeons learned to adapt and improvise.

In March, 1913, Louis C. Duncan, Captain in the Medical Corps of the U.S. Army, wrote an article for the journal, "*The Military Surgeon*," entitled "Evolution of the Ambulance Corps and Field Hospital." He concludes his article with this narrative:

> Whenever a column operated against the enemy, whenever sabers flashed or musketry rattled, there were ambulances ready to take up the wounded and swiftly convey them to the waiting hospitals in the rear. That these men did not wait for the bullets to cease flying is evidenced by the forty medical officers who died on the field of battle. Through the pines of Georgia and the swamps of the Carolinas; in the deadly thickets of the Wilderness and on the fire swept flats of Cold Harbor; in the last race with Meade and Sheridan; through rain and mud; over bottomless roads and across unbridged streams, the ambulance trains pressed on and the field hospitals were not far behind. No more wounded were abandoned on the field.
>
> By day and night, in mud and dust, in sun and storm, worked the officers and men of the medical department; without hope of reward or even official recognition. Noncombatants, they had not the urging of martial music nor the sweeping spirit of the charge to carry them on to duty. But laboring alone in the rear, often by night, and after days of exhausting toil, unseen and unchronicled, faithfully they performed their task; one requiring as rare a brand of courage as that which sends men to the cannon's mouth.[78]

Dispatch from Headquarters of the Army of Northern Virginia, May 6, 1863.

To Major General Joseph Hooker - Commanding General of the Army of the Potomac:

General, I have had the honor to receive your letter of yesterday, requesting permission to send a burial party to attend to your dead and wounded on the battlefield of Chancellorsville . I regret that their position is such, being immediately within our lines, that the necessities of war forbid my compliance with your request, which, under other circumstances, it would give me pleasure to grant. I will bestow to your dead and wounded the same attention which I bestow upon my own; but if there is anything which your medical director here requires which we cannot provide, he shall have my permission to receive from you such medical supplies as you think proper to furnish.

Consideration for your wounded prompts me to add that, from what I learn, their comfort would be greatly promoted by additional medical attendance and medical supplies.

I have the honor to be, respectfully, your obedient servant,
ROBERT E. LEE

- From *War of the Rebellion: A Compilation of the Official Records of the Union and Confederate Armies.*

PART 3

SURGICAL AND MEDICAL
PRACTICES
OF THE
CIVIL WAR

I - INTRODUCTION

When one thinks of Civil War medicine, the image of a surgeon, his apron covered in blood, performing amputation after amputation, comes immediately to mind. There is no doubt, amputation was the most commonly performed surgical procedure of the Civil War. In fact, Civil War doctors are almost always referred to as Civil War surgeons, in emphasis of the vast amount of surgery they performed. Of course, we know that these physicians treated many more cases of medical illness than they did actual war wounds. Of the 600,000 soldiers who died as a result of the conflict, two-thirds died from disease, and only one-third on the battlefield, or from wounds sustained in battle. However, when one ponders the mortality of the Civil War, the imagination conjures up the picture of a young soldier - dying "in glory and honor" - on the battlefield; not a soldier confined to a hospital bed, slowly drifting away from dehydration, with intractable vomiting and diarrhea. By the same token, one also envisions the Civil War surgeon repairing lacerations, applying tourniquets, removing bullets, and cutting off mangled limbs; not making rounds through a hospital ward, moving from bed to bed, passing out medications, and comforting sick soldiers.

Treating medically ill soldiers was a very important part of the physician's job. In all, it occupied much more time than the frantic hours after a battle when the acute surgical cases came rolling in. No doubt, between battles, hours, days, and weeks were spent caring for soldiers recuperating from their wounds or surgery, but at least as important, was the time spent caring for the sick soldiers who presented to daily sick call, or seriously ill soldiers in the various wards of the general hospitals.

As soldiers were massed in large numbers into small camps, infectious illness became a significant problem. Common childhood diseases such as measles, mumps, rubella, and chicken pox ran rampant, as soldiers were exposed to diseases for which they'd developed no prior immunity. Crowded conditions led to outbreaks of gastroenteritis, tuberculosis, pneumonia, malaria, typhoid fever, and other infectious illnesses. The civilian doctors, who later would become Civil War surgeons, had cared for these medical illnesses (albeit, not in such large numbers) in their private practices.

However, it is an indisputable fact, that in an army at war, surgical knowledge, skill and expertise come to the forefront. Civilian surgery involved relatively minor procedures such as lancing boils, pulling teeth, repairing lacerations, removing foreign bodies from the eye, and the like. Splints were applied to treat broken bones. Actual surgery was confined primarily to a few obstetrical and gynecological procedures. "Bleeding" or therapeutic blood letting was still practiced by some. However, even before the war, this practice was becoming less common.

Civilian injuries were produced in the home, on the farm, or in factories. Injuries resulted from falls, horseback riding, wagon mishaps, or accidents involving farm equipment or industrial machinery. Most gunshot wounds involved hunting arms such as shotguns or smoothbore muskets. A few were caused by handguns. These injuries were generally minor; major trauma was a rare and isolated occurrence.

The Civil War changed all that. As we have seen, the use of the rifled musket and minie ball, coupled with large numbers of soldiers involved in massed infantry charges, produced injuries of the type and quantity to immediately make necessary significant advances in the practice of surgical medicine. As previously described, textbooks were written, medical conventions held, case reports documented and studied, and individual physician experience was passed by word-of-mouth. As more experience accumulated, journal articles were written to disseminate information. The Sanitary Commission distributed pamphlets with their opinions regarding the subjects of surgical and medical practice.

Nearly 20,000 doctors, on both sides of the conflict, would be transformed from rural general practitioners into a new breed of physician, one that has come to define the medical practitioner of that war; the Civil War surgeon.

II - CIVIL WAR SURGERY

Prior to the Civil War, the smoothbore round-ball was the most commonly fired military projectile. The smoothbore round-ball more or less "lobbed" its way to its target, hitting with a dull smack. This usually produced a large contusion at the site of impact, and blunt trauma to the underlying muscle; often never breaking the skin. If it hit hard enough to break bone, the bone often split cleanly, rather than shattering. Commonly, the skin over the fractured bone would be left intact. Penetrating injury resulted when impact occurred at very close range.

A minie ball was a different beast altogether. The minie ball was a large, soft lead projectile with a conical shape. Its path down a rifled barrel imparted spin, and coupled with its shape, it had a long, flat trajectory. It was a powerful missile and often hit a soldier with devastating effect. This bullet tore through clothing, skin, and muscle. Bones in its path were smashed and fragmented into pieces. As the bullet hit bone, it flattened and distorted into bizarre shapes, or broke into pieces, each in turn tearing its way through the tissues. Often, clothing would be carried into a wound, contaminating it with dirt and debris. Many times, the projectile would carry away enough bone and soft tissue so as to nearly amputate an extremity instantaneously. Other times, massive trauma would occur to major nerves and blood vessels, making an extremity immediately useless and non-salvageable. Significant injuries to the head, chest, or abdomen were almost always fatal.

Effective management of this type of gunshot wound was a difficult task within the confines of surgical knowledge at the time of the Civil War. Even by today's standards, treatment of these devastating injuries would be a difficult matter.

For the hundreds of thousands of Civil War casualties, the Civil War occurred at an inopportune moment in the history of medicine. Serious injuries forced surgeons to perform invasive operative procedures - made possible by the availability of general anesthetics - with no attempt made to maintain aseptic (sterile) technique.

The anesthetic effects of ether were first demonstrated by a Boston dentist, William T.G. Morton, at Massachusetts General Hospital in 1846. Ether is a highly flammable substance, which makes it somewhat dangerous to use, particularly at a time when surgical lighting was provided by lantern or candle. Chloroform was introduced in 1847, by Scottish obstetrician James Simpson. Chloroform is nonflammable making it safer to use.

Prior to 1846, anesthesia had involved sedation with opium, morphine, or alcohol. To produce unconsciousness, such large amounts of these drugs had to be given that the patient often quit breathing, resulting in a fatal outcome. Ether and chloroform produce unconsciousness at levels that allow a patient to continue breathing. Both were extensively utilized during the Civil War. These anesthetics ushered in the capability to perform more advanced surgical procedures than ever before possible.

Unfortunately, Joseph Lister's theories concerning surgical antisepsis would not be accepted into standard medical practice for another decade. Combining general anesthesia with septic surgical technique produced disastrous results. The incidence of wound infection was horrific. After surviving major surgical procedures, thousands of soldiers died from subsequent post-operative wound infections. What today seems to be common sense sterile surgical procedure, never even entered the minds of most Civil War surgeons.

Be that as it may, the surgeons were presented with huge numbers of devastating casualties, and they did their best, using their best judgment and techniques of the day, to care for them as well as anyone could expect.

Most surgical procedures were performed in the field hospital. It was believed that major operations should be performed before the "irritative stage" (i.e., infection) began, which usually started between 24 to 48 hours after the wound was incurred.[79] Letterman ordered that, "each operating surgeon will be provided with an excellent table from the hospital wagon, and, with the present organization for field hospitals, it is hoped that the confusion and delay in performing the necessary operations so often existing after a battle be avoided, and all operations hereafter be primary."[80] In contrast, secondary surgery was performed more than 24 to 48 hrs. after the wound had occurred, in the hope that some limbs would prove to be viable, even if they did not appear so initially. Civil War statistics showed that the overall mortality for primary amputation was 28%; mortality for secondary amputation was 52%.[81] The standard practice of the Civil War was to perform surgery as a primary operation, as soon as possible after the injury had occurred.

Conservative treatment, with attempt at limb salvage rather than amputation, was becoming more popular in civilian practice. By nature, civilian injuries tended to be cleaner and less destructive to bone and other tissues. Also, these wounds tended to occur as isolated cases. Time could be taken to inspect, clean, and repair these injuries. In contrast, military surgeons had to deal quickly with huge numbers of casualties, resulting in less time for careful exploration, cleaning, and repair of individual wounds.

The surgical protocol of the Civil War was fairly straight-forward. As the wounded arrived to the field hospital, anesthetics were quickly administered, and the amputations began. Doses of liquor were given in an attempt to revive patients in shock. The mortally wounded were placed in a comfortable place, medicated to relieve pain, and allowed to die. After surgery, arrangements were made to transport the post-operative patients to a general hospital for recuperation. Patients were moved quickly out of field facilities, to make way for the next wave of wounded arriving from the battlefield.

In terms of equipment, the Civil War surgeon had many, basic instruments at his disposal. Each surgeon and assistant surgeon carried his own pocket surgical kit. Some carried more than one. The exact instruments contained within the kit varied by individual physician, based on personal preference. The case was usually made out of leather and was divided into two or three sections. The folded kit measured about 6 inches long and 3 to 4 inches wide. Inside, it might contain several scalpels (convexly curved surgical knives), bistouries (straight or concavely curved surgical knives), scissors (surgical and dressing), forceps (tissue and arterial), thumb lancets (to incise small abcesses or for bleeding), gum lancets (to aid in tooth extraction), exploring needles and probes, silk suture and suture needles, small foreign body or bullet extractors, and trochars (hollow tubes, inserted over needles, to drain deep abcesses). The surgical knives often folded into ivory or tortoise shell handles for compactness. Each kit also contained metal catheters to drain the urinary bladder.

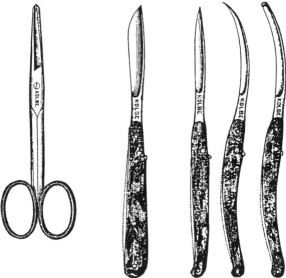

Figure 4: Scissors, Scalpel (center), Bistouries (3 instruments on right)

Each physician carried only the instruments that he felt necessary and used frequently. As Dr. Stephen Smith states in the "*Handbook of Surgical Operations*," published in 1862, "A case may be selected which contains all the instruments ordinarily required in every-day practice, and which occupies so little space in the pocket as to become a constant companion without the slightest inconvenience."[82]

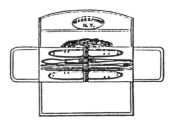

Figure 5: A small pocket case of instruments

Operating surgeons also had a "general operating case" of instruments. These were used to perform major surgeries. A field hospital may have had only one such kit; a general hospital may have had several. Some of these surgical kits belonged to the individual physician and had been used in his civilian practice. More commonly, the U.S. Army provided each regimental surgeon with a general operating case and these were the ones most often utilized.

The general cases were made by various manufacturers so their design varied. The actual case was a wooden box, often made of oak, walnut, or mahogany. The dimensions of the box varied by the size of the kit. Most were about 12 to 18 inches long, 6 or 7 inches wide, and 2 to 4 inches deep. The box was divided into sections by removable wooden trays. The box and trays were lined with velvet, with compartments and indentations designed to precisely hold individual instruments. Some kits were quite large, and contained instruments in the top and bottom of the case, as well as in one or more removable trays. Others contained instruments only in the top and bottom of the case itself. Specialized surgical kits were issued that contained instruments required solely for amputation, trephining (cranial surgery), or exsection (surgical removal of isolated sections of damaged bone).

Frank Hastings Hamilton, M.D. was a well-respected surgeon at the time of the Civil War. While serving with the Thirty-First Infantry of New York, he was in charge of a field hospital at the First Battle of Bull Run. In 1861, he authored, "*A Practical Treatise on Military Surgery*"; one of the standard military medicine references of the day.[83]

The contents of Dr. Hamilton's surgical case were typical of a general operating case:

> One long amputating knife; one amputating knife; one catling; two small amputating knives; one metacarpal saw; one large saw; one bone forceps; one tenaculum; one short bistoury, sharp; one pair slide artery forceps; one pair bull-dog artery forceps; one pair large scissors; one pair small scissors; one pair dressing forceps; one long silver bullet probe; one whalebone bullet probe; one small silver probe; two dozen serrefines; two dozen needles; one tourniquet, screw; one tourniquet, field; one director; one conical trephine; one elevator; one Hay's saw; one brush; three bullet forceps; two retractors; one needle forceps; one plain aneurysm needle; one set Dr. Mott's needles; silk and silver wire. Dimensions: seventeen inches long, nine inches wide, two and a half inches deep.[84]

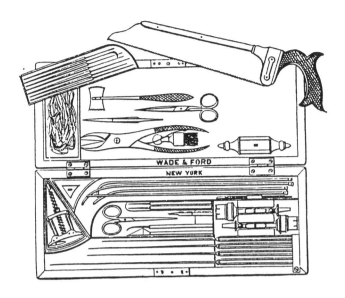

Figure 6: A typical general operating case of instruments

Pocket surgical kits and general surgical cases were made by many different manufacturers. In the U.S., most medical instrument supply firms were located in the North. These companies included Geo. Tiemann & Co., New York; Hernstein & Co., New York; Shepard & Dudley, New York; Max Wocher & Son, Cincinnati, Ohio, and others. Each manufacturer stamped their name on the kit or case for identification.

The South relied on captured Union stores to supply their medical equipment needs, or had instruments shipped from Europe, through the Union blockade. Many pocket kits and surgical cases were obtained from England or France. Overseas manufacturers included J. Weiss, London; Ferguson, London; Mathieu, Paris; Charrierre, Paris, and others.

The nature and types of wounds produced by gunshot and other projectiles are determined by factors related to the projectile itself, and where and how that projectile strikes the body.

A wide variety of military projectiles is reviewed by Dr. Charles Tripler in his "*Hand-Book for the Military Surgeon*", "Projectiles, or other bodies inflicting wounds in battle, are generally buckshot, musket, pistol, or rifle balls, canister, solid or hollow round shot, grape, fragments of shell or stone, splinters from gun carriages, etc. Of late years, the smooth bore muskets and spherical balls have fallen into disuse. The improved rifled barrels, and the conical (minie) ball have superseded them almost entirely."[85]

While all of these projectiles, as well as saber and bayonet, produced Civil War injuries, the vast majority of wounds were produced by bullets. Statistically, it has been determined that 94% of wounds were inflicted by bullets, 5.5% by artillery fire and grenades, and less than 1% by saber or bayonet. In a study of 144,000 cases of gunshot wounds where the type of missile could be ascertained, the minie ball caused 108,000 wounds, the smoothbore round-ball caused 16,000.[86] Artilllery fire accounted for the remainder. Obviously, the Civil War surgeon was dealing primarily with bullet wounds inflicted by the minie ball.

The site of a gunshot injury is determined by the body position of the soldier at the moment he is shot. A firing soldier, when standing, exposes the top of his head; his left arm is outstretched exposing the primarily the hand; the forearm and upper arm are presented in the long axis, producing very little target area; the right arm, with the right index finger on the trigger, extends out to the side exposing a larger target area of the forearm and also the upper arm. The body is turned to the side exposing the left side of the chest and abdomen; the left side of the pelvis and the entire left leg are also exposed. Depending on the degree of rotation and the direction of travel of the projectile, some of the right pelvis and lower extremity may also be exposed.

A soldier firing from a kneeling position exposes the upper extremities in a similar fashion. However, the left elbow rests on the knee exposing much more of the left forearm. The left lower leg is exposed much more than the left upper leg. With the right knee on the ground, the right lower leg is protected and the upper leg exposed. The chest and abdomen are protected by the left arm and leg.

A prone shooter, or one protected by breastworks, exposes little but the head and upper extremities.

A soldier, loading a muzzle-loading weapon, tends to stand or kneel in the position from which he fired; facing rightward, continuing to predominantly expose the left side of the body.

The above factors resulted in a majority of injuries to the left side of the body.

From statistics compiled after the war, the following relative frequency of anatomic locations of gunshot wounds was noted;[87]

Head and Neck	10.77%
Trunk	18.37%
Upper Extremities	35.71%
Lower Extremities	35.15%

Chest and abdominal injuries were particularly dangerous and difficult to manage in the preantiseptic era. Gunshot wounds to the head are difficult injuries in any era. The soldiers may be considered "fortunate" in that 71% of their injuries involved the extremities.

In a study of 44,000 Union soldiers reported as "killed in action", referring to those actually found dead on the battlefield, 82% showed evidence of wounds to the head, chest or neck; 12% showed evidence of wounds to the abdomen; only 5% showed evidence of fatal wounds to the extremities (presumably due to injuries involving major arteries, resulting in massive blood loss).[88]

EXTREMITY TRAUMA AND AMPUTATIONS:

Amputation was the most common major surgical procedure of the war. It has been estimated that approximately 50,000 amputations were performed; North and South combined. Confederate statistics are incomplete; for the Union the following statistics have been reported.[89]

UNION AMPUTATIONS

Region	Cases	Deaths	% Fatalities
Fingers	7,900	198	3
Forearm	1,700	245	14
Upper Arm	6,500	1,273	24
Toes	1,500	81	6
Lower Leg	5,500	1,700	38
Middle Thigh	6,300	3,411	54
Knee Joint	195	111	58
Hip Joint	66	55	88

As was mentioned previously, it was generally believed that major operations should be performed as soon as possible after the wound was received. These amputations usually took place in the field hospitals.

When news arrived that a major engagement was about to take place, surgeons selected buildings to serve as field hospitals, and the preparations began. Clyde B. Kerneck, M.D. provides the following fictional narrative in his book, "*Field Surgeon at Gettysburg*:"[90]

> Doors had been pulled off hinges and placed on boxes and barrels to serve as makeshift operating tables. Stewards were working hard to set out amputation sets and bandages on tables for instant use.
> Chloroform, tincture of opium, and morphine sulfate solution in glass vials were neatly lined up on tables. Large tin medicine containers of spirits fermenti were also set out, but had to be guarded as this hospital alcohol was much sought out for nonmedical uses.
> The surgeons assembling in the farm house were nerved but anxious, expecting mass casualties.

Before long ambulances were arriving and the casualties came pouring in,

The smell of chloroform permeated the house. All of the windows were wide open for ventilation, and gnats were swarming about the candlelight. The small tables about the rooms were completely covered with surgical instruments and rolls of muslin bandages, and long amputating knives and bone saws with their handles protruding sat in pans of bloody water, ready to be grabbed by the busy surgeons. Orderlies and attendants were amazingly efficient in the dispatch of their duties, toting and carrying human cargo as if they were dockhands. They bore the wounded men into the house and took the treated and dead out to the yard and barn.

Soon, in the dim candlelight, a screaming soldier was placed on a table. "Gunshot wound to the right elbow", an orderly said. "It's shattered the humerus at the elbow joint." Amputation was needed immediately.

Surgeon Zabdiel Adams and Assistant Surgeons, Theodore St. James and Morgan E. Baldwin immediately went to work. As Baldwin relates:

Adams began by pouring the chloroform upon a handkerchief folded into the shape of a cup. He instructed the terrified patient to take slow, deep breaths and gradually brought the handkerchief closer to the man's mouth and nose...in about five minutes the struggling man was only able to whimper. I applied the tourniquet as high up the arm as possible and tightened it. An attendant secured the forearm while I held the upper arm. St. James reached for a long Catling amputating knife, sharp on both edges, with a sharp point on the end. ...He plunged the knife through the center of the arm midway between the elbow and the shoulder. He cut a flap of tissue from inside out on the front of the upper arm. The wounded soldier's fingers quivered as the long knife stimulated and divided the nerves in the arm. Just as quickly, St. James cut the back flap and told me to grab the bloody flaps with my fingers and pull them up the arm. The humerus was then widely exposed, and he quickly scraped the remaining soft tissues from the bone. ... St. James grabbed the capital bone saw. He cut the humerus with rapid saw strokes. As soon as the bone had been divided, the limb was free. St. James threw the amputated arm out the open window.
I continued to retract the skin flaps while St. James hooked the brachial artery with a tenaculum and ligated it with silk thread. ...I released the tourniquet, ...St. James sponged the bleeding muscle to remove clots and blood, and the small bleeders were controlled with pressure. In a few minutes the flaps had been approximated with several widely spaced silk sutures. Adhesive straps were placed on the skin between the sutures. A dressing was applied by placing a pad of folded flannel over the surgical wound and wrapping a muslin bandage roll over this pad and about the amputation stump and upper arm. Adams let the patient awaken from the anesthesia while the bandage was being applied. "When are you going to cut off my arm?", the groggy soldier asked.

51

The septic conditions under which these amputations were performed is described by General Carl Schurz describing a scene at a field hospital after the Battle of Gettysburg:

> There stood the surgeons, their sleeves rolled up to their elbows, their bare arms as well as their linen aprons smeared with blood, their knives not seldom held between their teeth ... a wounded man was lifted on the table ... the surgeon snatched his knife from between his teeth..., wiped it rapidly once or twice across his bloodstained apron, and the cutting began. The operation accomplished, the surgeon would look around with a deep sigh, and then-"Next!"[91]

Dr. Kerneck's narrative describes the flap-type of amputation. Amputations were also performed using the circular technique.

As Dr. Stephen Smith describes in his "*Handbook of Surgical Operations*"; the three principle steps involved in the circular amputation method are; 1-Incision of the skin; 2-Incision of the muscles; 3-Section of the bone. 1-The skin is incised with a single edged amputating knife drawn with a circumferential stroke around the limb. The skin is raised from the first layer of muscles by dissection, and drawn upwards, two or three inches, according to the diameter of the limb, like the cuff of a coat. 2-The first layer of muscles is divided at the margins of the retracted skin, in the same manner as the incision of the skin is executed; this layer is raised with the knife, and drawn still further upwards; and the last layer of muscles is divided down to the bone. 3-The bone is then sawn at the apex of the cone.[92] Arteries and large veins were then drawn out of the stump using forceps, and ligated with silk or cotton thread. Nerves were drawn out, transected, and allowed to retract into the stump. The stump was then closed with sutures and/or adhesive plaster and a dressing was applied.

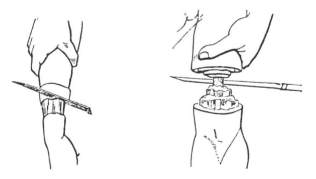

Figure 7: Circular Method of Amputation.
A single-edged amputation knife was used for
this operation.

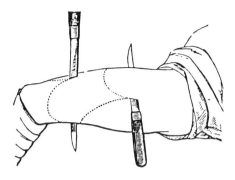

Figure 8: Flap-type Amputation. The diagram illustrates two possible incisions.
The leftward incision would produce medial and lateral flaps;
the rightward incision would produce anterior and posterior flaps.
A double-edged (or Catling) amputation knife was used for this operation.

Both the flap and circular types of amputation were used throughout the war. Each technique had it's advantages and disadvantages. The relative advantages or disadvantages particular to each method were debated among surgeons. In general, the circular method was easier to dress, easier to transport, and may have produced fewer cases of secondary hemorrhage. The advantages of the flap method included the speed in which it could be performed and the larger amount of soft tissue retained to cover the bone.[93]

Dr. Samuel David Gross, in "*A Manual of Military Surgery*," published in 1861, makes his case for the flap technique:

> Little need be said here about the methods of amputation. In cases of emergency, where time is precious, and the number of surgeons inadequate, the flap operation deserves, in my opinion, a decided preference over the circular...the rapidity with which it may be executed, the abundant covering which it affords for the bone, and the facility with which the parts unite are qualities which strongly recommend it to the judgment of the military surgeon.[94]

Another technique utilized in amputation is disarticulation. Using this technique an amputation is performed by cutting the tissues through a joint; this requires no sawing of bone. Fingers, or portions of them, and toes were often removed by this procedure.

Amputation, as described above, was the most common method used to remove a limb. A technique was also used whereby the limb was surgically opened, the shattered bone removed, and the skin closed; resulting in retention of the limb. This operation is known as exsection (or resection). This procedure required a very skillful surgeon, with a detailed knowledge of anatomy. To be considered treatable by this procedure, the injury had to have resulted in relatively isolated bone damage. There had to be little damage to the surrounding muscles, nerves, and major blood vessels. The procedure was quite time consuming when compared to amputation. Obviously, this technique played a somewhat limited role in the overall practice of Civil War surgery. Excision was most often attempted at the wrist, shoulder, elbow, and ankle.

In this procedure, the wound was meticulously examined for foreign material and evidence of trauma to major nerves or blood vessels. The skin was incised and careful dissection through muscles, tendons, nerves, and arteries was performed. The damaged bone was exposed and dissected along it's length, in each direction, to expose non-traumatized proximal and distal portions. Using a saw - often a chain saw that could be looped around the bone - the damaged bone was "resected" and removed. The soft tissues and skin were then closed and a dressing and splint applied. The postoperative infection rate was higher than with amputation, and the hospitalization period and rehabilitative phases were much longer. The ultimate result was a shortened limb with more or less retention of function, depending on the initial injury and healing process. Often, at the site of the operation, a pseudoarthrosis (false joint) occurred. For many soldiers, this procedure resulted in the retention of a useful limb; much preferred to amputation. For others, the limb was relatively useless and difficult to manage. A few subsequently underwent amputation of the useless limb to allow for the fitting of a functional prosthesis.

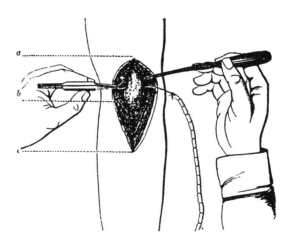

Figure 9: Example of a Resection
Note the chain saw being positioned under the bone

Besides amputation or resection, gunshot wounds could also be managed conservatively. This method of treatment involved careful examination of the wound for significant injuries to major arteries, nerves, or bone - which would necessitate amputation. If none were found, the wound was cleaned of foreign material, debrided of devitalized tissue, and repaired and dressed. In his "*Handbook of Surgical Operations*", Dr. Smith describes the procedure:

- On arrival at the hospital, the following are the points to be attended to by the surgeon: firstly, examination of the wound with a view to obtaining a correct knowledge of its nature and extent; secondly, removal of any foreign bodies which may have lodged; thirdly, adjustment of lacerated structures; and fourthly, the application of the primary dressings.

- One of the earliest rules for examining a gunshot wound is to place the patient...in a position similar to that in which he was, in relation to the missile, at the time of being struck by it....The examination will be facilitated by attention to this precept.

- When only one opening has been made by a ball, it is to be presumed that it is lodged somewhere in the wound, and search must be made for it accordingly. ...Even where two openings exist, examination should still be made to detect the presence of foreign bodies. Portions of clothing, and other harder substances, are not infrequently carried into a wound...

- Of all instruments for conducting an examination of a gunshot wound, the finger of the surgeon is most appropriate. The index finger naturally occurs as the most convenient for this employment; but the opening through the skin is sometimes too contracted to admit its entrance, and in this case the substitution of the little finger will usually answer all the purposes intended.

- It does not often happen that it is necessary to enlarge the openings of wounds to remove balls...if much resistance is offered to their passage out, it is better to divide the edges of the fascia and skin to the amount of enlargement required than to use force.

-Where the finger is not sufficiently long to reach the bottom of the wound... a long silver probe, that admits of being bent by hand, is the best substitute.

- As soon as the presence of a ball or other foreign body is ascertained it should be removed...by means of some of the various instruments devised for the purpose.

-When a gunshot wound has been accompanied with much laceration and disturbance of the parts involved in the injury, it is necessary, after removal of all foreign substances that can be detected, to readjust and secure the disjointed structures as nearly as possible in their normal relations to each other. The simplest means - strips of adhesive plaster, light pledgets of moist lint, a linen roller...should be adopted for this purpose.[95]

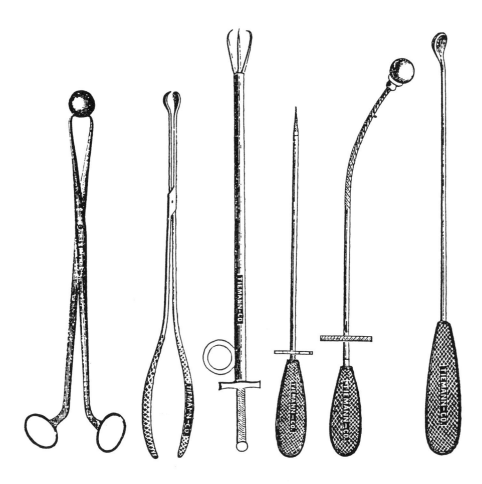

Figure 10: Various Types of Bullet Extractors

The conservative approach was most often used in treatment of hand and wrist injuries; due to better healing and retention of function. It was also used in the treatment of wounds to the hip and proximal femur; due to the high mortality associated with surgical intervention in those areas. Amputations through the femur, near the hip, or resections near the hip, produced mortalities of 83% and 91%, respectively, so neither was recommended.[96] However, even with conservative treatment, the mortality was 82%, so the chance of surviving these devastating injuries was slim, no matter what treatment method was employed.

Tabulating statistics on approximately 30,000 gunshot wounds to the extremities of Union soldiers; 49.4% were treated with amputation (approximately 60% by the flap-type of procedure); 11.3% were treated with excision; 39.3% were treated in a conservative fashion.[97]

HEAD AND NECK TRAUMA:

Injuries to the head and neck area accounted for 10.77% of Civil War gunshot wounds. Many of these injuries resulted in death on the battlefield. Head wounds were categorized into those which just involved the scalp, and those which involved the cranium and its contents. The treatment of gunshot wounds to the head had not changed for many years. Trephination, or the boring of a hole through the skull to reduce intracranial pressure, was a procedure that had been used since Egyptian times. In his "*Handbook of Surgical Operations*," Dr. Smith states, "Injuries of this class, the most slight in appearance at their outset, not infrequently prove most grave as they proceed, from encephalitis and its consequences...to coma, paralysis, or pyemia."[98] He goes on to discuss the specifics of treatment:

-Wounds of the Scalp and Pericranium: Cleansing the surface of the wound, removing hair from its neighborhood for the easier application of dressings, lint moistened with clean water, very spare diet, and careful regulation of the excretions, are the only requirements in most cases. Even in these accidents, though appearing to be simple flesh wounds, serious cerebral concussion and other lesions are occasionally met with.

- Wounds Complicated with Fracture, but without Depression on the Cerebrum: ...Such injuries are very likely to be followed by inflammation, and not improbably abcess, between the inner table and the dura mater. ...In cases where comminution has occurred...the small, loose fragments can be removed.

-Wounds Complicated with Fracture and Depression on the Cerebrum: Such wounds are most serious, and the prognosis must be very unfavorable. Gunshot wounds cause severe concussion of the whole osseous sphere by the stroke of the projectile, with bruising and injury of the bony texture immediately surrounding the spot against which it has impinged, as well as the contusion of the external soft parts....So, also, the injury to the brain within, and its investments, is greater.

- Wounds with Penetration of the Cerebrum: It is obvious that, where a projectile has power not only to fracture, but also to penetrate the cranium, it will rarely be arrested in its progress near the wound of entrance. Either splinters of bone, or the ball, or a portion of it will be carried through the membranes into the cerebral mass. ...The course a projectile may follow within the cranium is very uncertain.

-Treatment: Modern surgeons generally have made use of the trephine only when there was reason for concluding that depressed bone was leading to permanent interruption of cerebral function, or that an abcess had formed within reach, and was capable of evacuation. Preventative trephining has been proved to be useless...and is no longer an admissible operation.

Most authors of military medical texts, at the time of the Civil War, included a chapter on the treatment of head injuries. Unless the injury was confined to the scalp, outcome was universally felt to be poor, regardless of treatment. Basically, the wound was cleaned of foreign debris, hair, and devitalized tissue. The wound was probed with the surgeon's finger. If the injury was confined to the scalp, sutures were placed to approximate skin edges, and dressings were applied. If the skull was fractured, loose pieces of bone were removed. A Hey's saw was a special tool used in cranial surgery to aid in the removal of pieces of fractured skull. Instruments called elevators were used to lift fragments of bone off the surface of the brain. The path of the projectile into the brain was probed with the surgeon's finger, and the ball removed if possible. Attempts to explore the wound with a metal probe, or dig deeply into the wound with bullet extractors, were felt to be dangerous and inappropriate. As Tripler writes, "If the ball has penetrated deeply into the brain, it is a matter of little moment what steps are taken; perhaps, however, it is the best line of conduct to let the man die in peace."[99]

The larger surgical cases contained the instruments necessary to perform cranial surgery. A special trephination case was also available. It contained a pair of trephines, a Hey's saw, a scalpel, bone elevators, and a brush. Some kits also contained a trepan. A trepan is a hole saw that is operated like a hand drill - by turning a crank. In contrast, a trephine is a hole saw that bores through the skull by using a twisting motion.

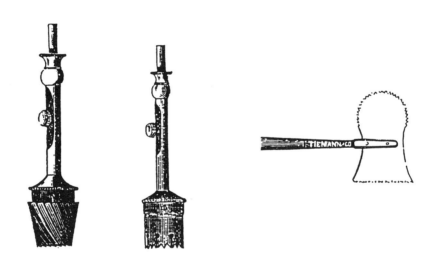

Figure 11: Examples of Trephines and a Hey's Saw

Civil War mortality statistics, regarding head wounds, are as follows: Superficial scalp lacerations - 1.5%; Fracture of the outer table of skull - 9%; Fracture of the outer and inner skull tables, but without penetration into the brain- 65%; Fractures of both tables, with minimal penetration into the brain - 86%; Fractures with significant penetration into the brain - 100%.[100]

Neck wounds were particularly dangerous due to the large number of vital structures confined to a small area. If the wounds were superficial, treatment was straight-forward and the outcome generally good. Minor lacerations to the large vessels would occasionally clot off. Styptics were used in an attempt to cauterize lacerated blood vessels. However, injuries to the deeper structures were difficult to treat and outcome was usually poor.

Vital structures in the neck include the carotid arteries, the jugular veins, the larynx and the trachea. Significant injury to one of these often resulted in death on the battlefield. Non-fatal injuries were difficult to manage and often produced permanent disability. Wounds involving the esophagus were not usually immediately fatal, but generally caused long-term problems with swallowing and feeding. Cervical spine injuries often resulted in early death secondary to paralysis of the respiratory muscles, or slow death from infection.

Trauma to the spinal column, anywhere along its length, was associated with significant morbidity and mortality. There was little hope for recovery from major trauma to the spinal cord. Secondary infection led to a high incidence of death from meningitis. Surgery was rarely performed except for superficial injuries, which probably did not have true spinal cord involvement, anyway. Mortality figures for spinal trauma were: cervical spine - 70.0%; thoracic spine - 63.5%; lumbar spine - 45.5%.[101]

CHEST TRAUMA:

Wounds to the chest are divided into two categories; non-penetrating and penetrating. Non-penetrating wounds consist of superficial contusions and lacerations to the chest wall, with or without rib fractures. A penetrating wound implies penetration of the parietal pleura (the membranous lining of the inside of the rib cage).

Dr. Smith describes the management of chest wounds:

> ...Among the more serious complications of the penetrating injury is the lodgment of the projectile or other foreign bodies, as of fragments of bone, within the chest. As wounds of the heart and great vessels are almost invariably at once fatal, and as the organs of respiration occupy the greater part of the cavity of this region, it is in reference to the latter that the treatment of chest wounds is chiefly concerned.
> -Non-Penetrating Wounds: When the force has been great, as when fragments of shell or rifle-balls strike at full speed against a man's breast-plate, not only may troublesome superficial abscesses and sinuses follow, but the lungs may have been compressed and ecchymosed at the time of the injury, and hemoptysis be one of the symptoms presented. ...Although the pleura has not been opened, the lung may be lacerated either by the force of contusion or by the edges of the fractured ribs...this will be indicated by emphysema, pneumothorax, hemoptysis, probably signs of internal hemorrhage, and inflammation.

-Penetrating Wounds: These wounds, especially when the lung is perforated or the projectile lodges, are necessarily exceedingly dangerous. Fatal consequences are to be feared, either from hemorrhage, leading to exhaustion or suffocation; from inflammation of the pulmonary structure or pleura; from irritative fever accompanying profuse discharges; or from fluid accumulations in one or both of the pleural sacs. When the chest has been opened by a projectile, the following signs may be expected in addition to the external physical evidences of the injury: a certain amount of constitutional shock; collapse from the loss of blood; and, if the lung be wounded, effusion into the pleural cavity, hemoptysis, dyspnea, and an exsanguine appearance. If air and frothy mucus with blood escape by the wound, there can be no doubt of the nature of the injury.

-Treatment: The object of the surgeon's care must be in the first place to arrest hemorrhage; afterwards, to remove pieces or jagged projections of bone, or any other sources of local irritation.
...Hemorrhage from vessels belonging to the costal parietes should be arrested by ligature...if the flow of blood cannot be controlled by local styptics. Hemorrhage from the lung itself must be treated on the general principles adopted in all such cases; the application of cold to the chest, perfect quiet, and the administration of opium...When blood has accumulated in any large quantity, and the patient is much oppressed, the wound should be enlarged, if necessary, so as, with the assistance of proper position, to facilitate its escape. If the effused blood, from the situation of the wound, cannot be thus evacuated, and the patient be in danger of suffocation, then the performance of paracentesis must be resorted to.
To remove splinters of bone, and readjust indented portions of the ribs, the finger should be introduced into the wound, and care taken that in doing so no pieces of cloth or fragments be separated and projected into the pleural sac. Notice must at the same time be taken of any bleeding vessel requiring to be secured. A pledget of lint should be laid over the wound, and a broad dressing placed round the chest...If the presence of a ball within the cavity be ascertained, efforts should be made for its removal. But any attempt to determine where the ball has lodged should be made very cautiously, as more harm may result from the interference than from the lodgment of the foreign body.

Wounds of the heart seldom come to the military surgeon's notice, as they ordinarily prove fatal on the battlefield.[102]

(Definitions - **ecchymosed**: bruised; **hemoptysis**: coughing up blood; **emphysema**: air in and under the skin; **pneumothorax**: air trapped between the lung and the rib cage; **dyspnea**: shortness of breath; **costal**: ribs; **exsanguine**: pale - due to loss of blood; **paracentesis**: removing blood or other fluid from the chest utilizing a trochar and hollow needle)

Fortunately, Civil War statistics reveal that more than 50% of chest wounds were superficial, with a mortality rate of about 1%. Union statistics document treatment of 8,700 penetrating chest wounds, with a mortality rate of 62%.[103]

Surgeon General William A. Hammond (Courtesy Library of Congress)

Dr. Jonathan Letterman (seated at left), Medical Director of the Army of the Potomac, and staff. (Courtesy Library of Congress)

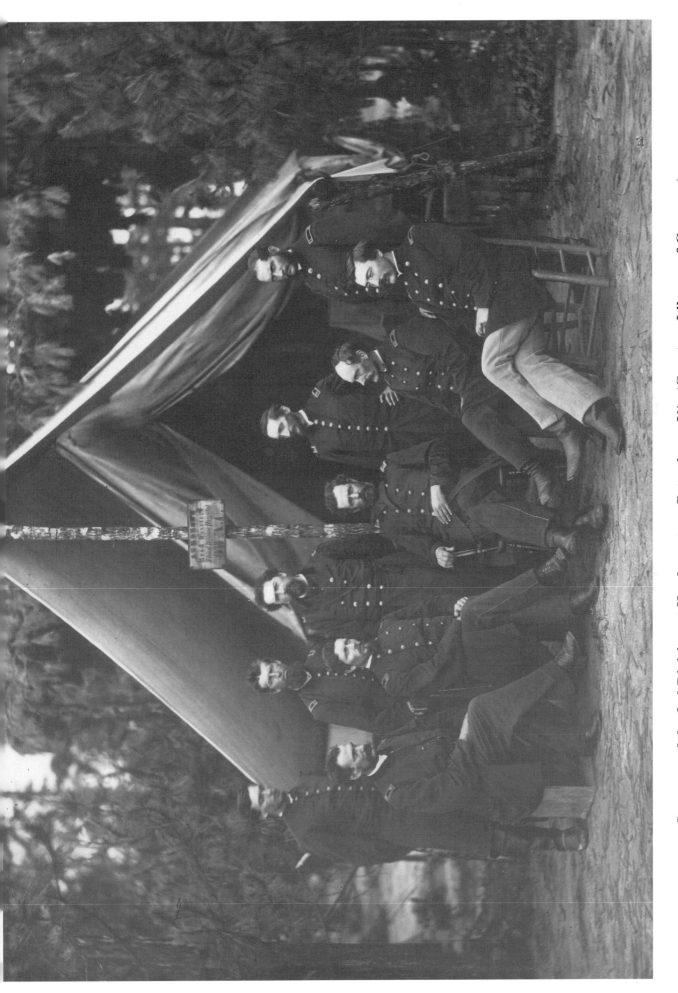

Surgeons of the 3rd Division at Headquarters, Petersburg, VA. (Courtesy Library of Congress)

Men and wagons of the Engineer Corps Ambulance Train (Courtesy Library of Congress)

Union Surgeon Dr. Anson Hurd, 14th Indiana Volunteers. Attending to Confederate wounded, behind the lines, in a field hospital after the Battle of Antietam. (Courtesy Library of Congress)

Field Hospital after the Battle of Savage Station, VA., June 27, 1862. (Courtesy Library of Congress)

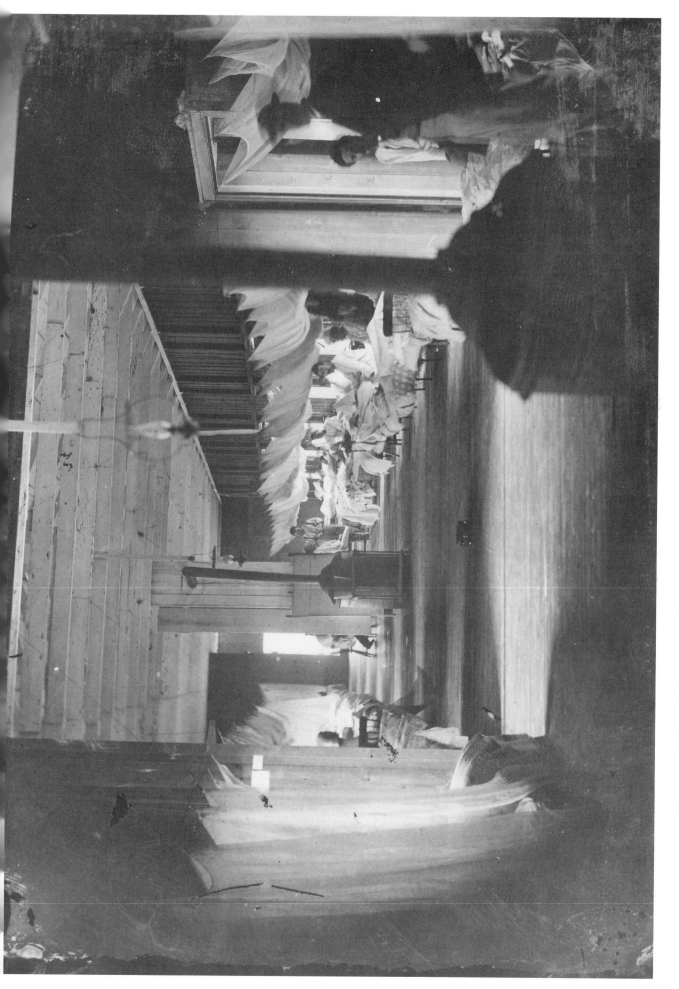

Harewood Hospital. A general hospital in Washington, D.C. (Courtesy Library of Congress)

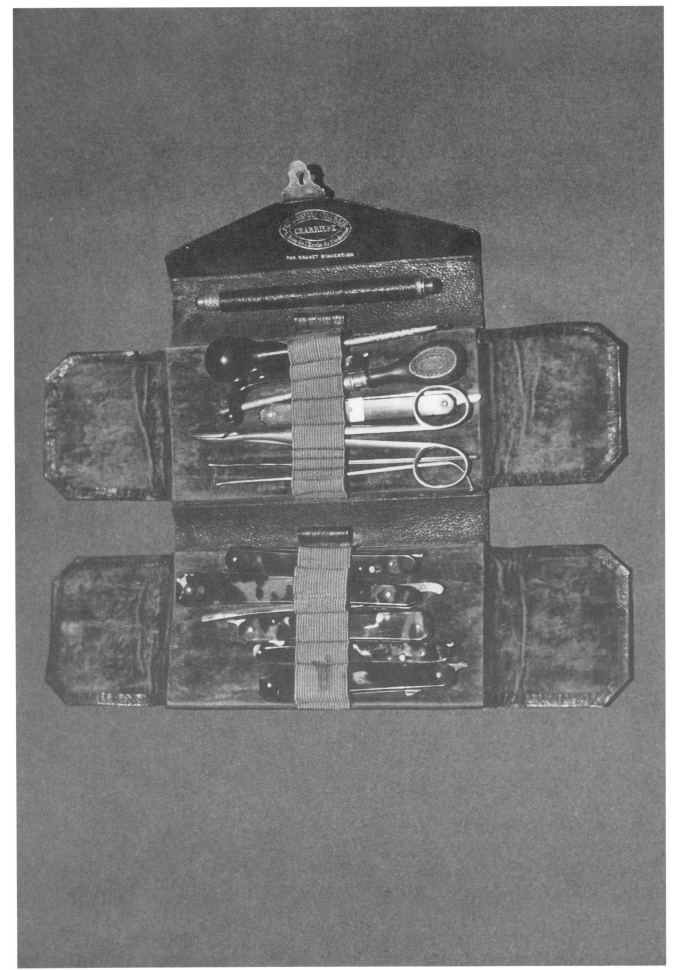

Pocket Surgical Kit (Author's collection)

Pocket Surgical Kit (Author's collection)

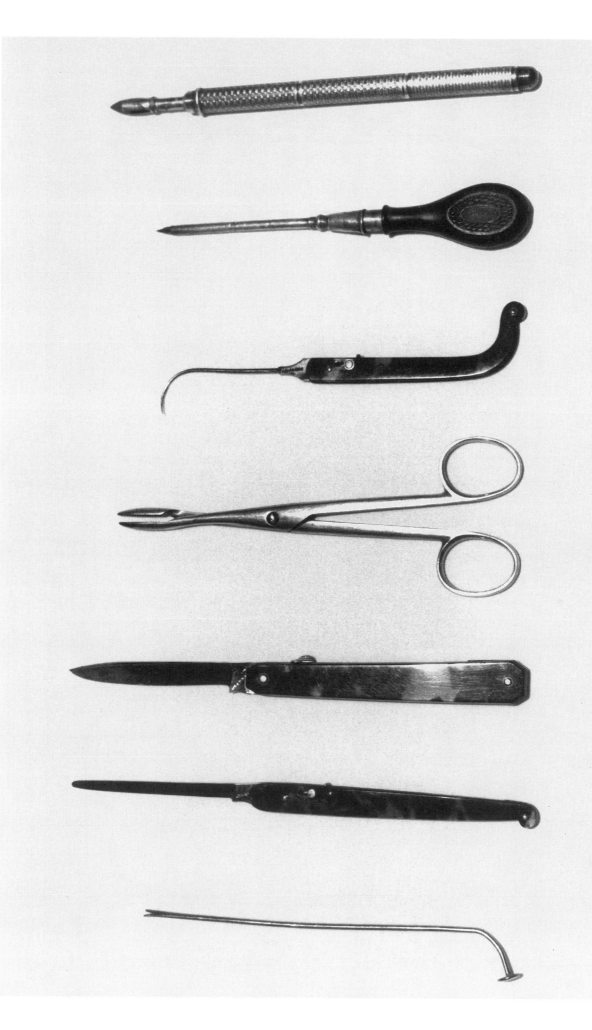

Instruments from a pocket kit. (L to R): suture guide; bistoury; scalpel; bullet extractor; tenaculum; trochar and cannula; styptic holder (Author's collection)

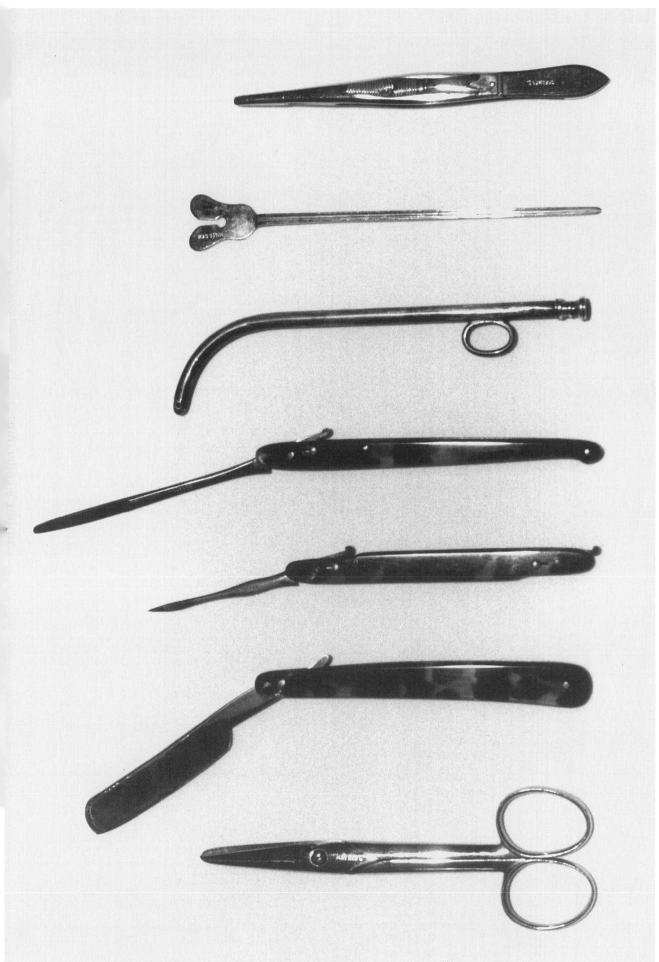

Instruments from a pocket kit. (L to R): scissors, three folding instruments with tortoise-shell handles: razor, scalpel, bistoury; urinary catheter; scalpel director; arterial forceps (Author's collection)

General Surgical Case (Author's collection)

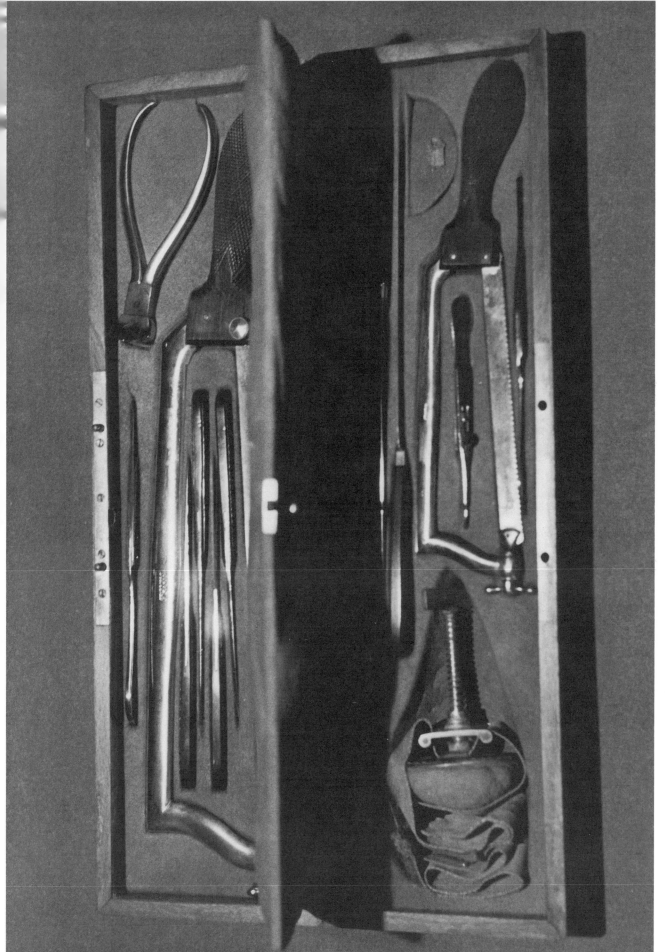

General Surgical Case showing instruments in top compartment.

Amputation knives (Author's collection)

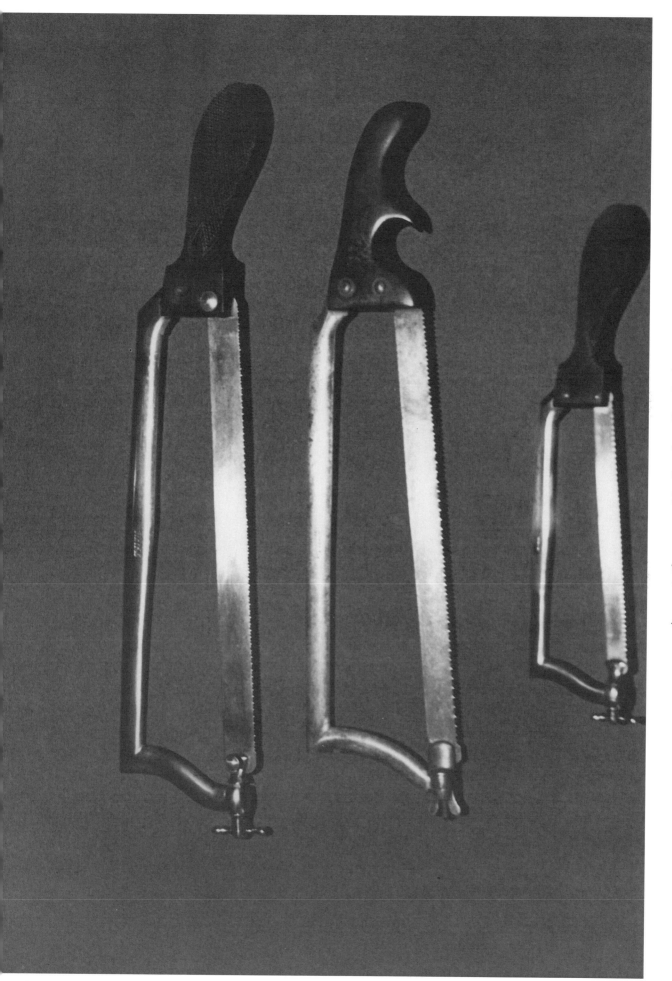

Amputation saws (Author's collection)

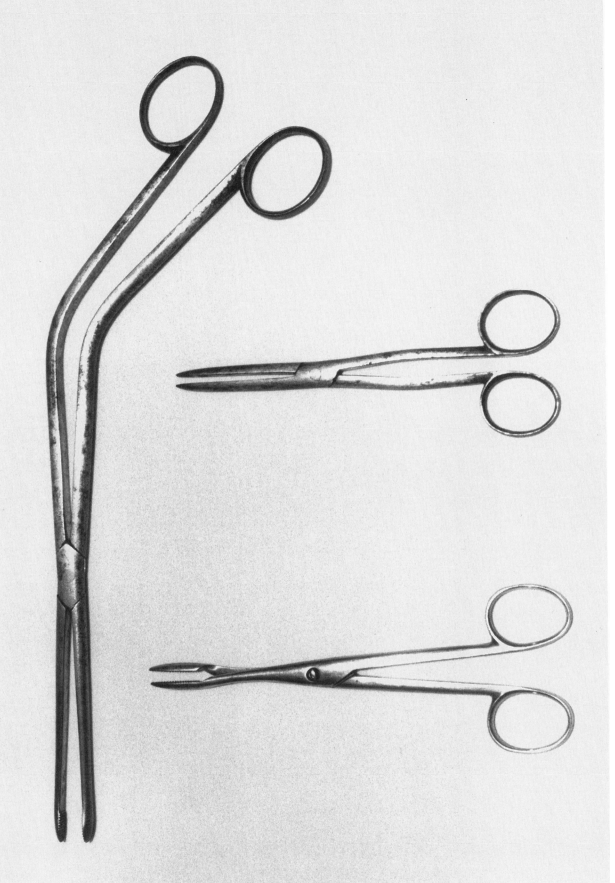

Foreign body/bullet extractors (Author's collection)

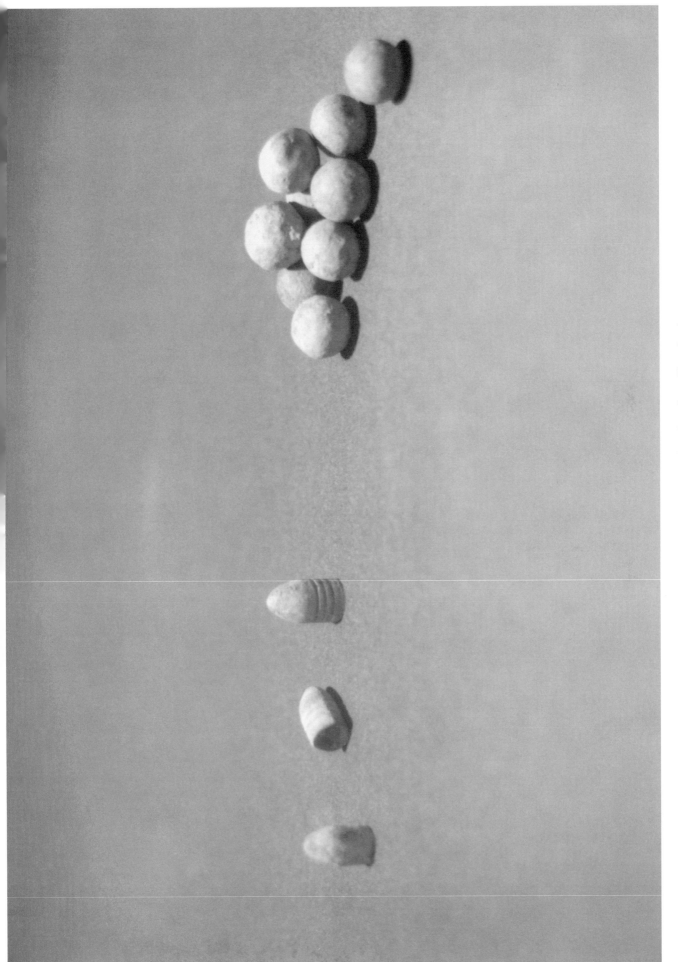

Minie balls and Grape shot (author's collection)

ABDOMINAL TRAUMA:

Wounds to the abdomen are divided into two categories; penetrating and non-penetrating. Non-penetrating injuries involve only the abdominal wall. Penetrating injuries are characterized by penetration of the peritoneum (parietes) - the membranous lining of the abdominal cavity - which contains the internal organs.

Dr. Smith describes their management:

-Non-Penetrating Wounds: If, although the viscera have been contused, the injury does not amount to being mortal, the patient should be subjected to perfect quiet, extreme abstinence, and, only when inflammation arises, to the necessary treatment for its control. If the parietes have been much contused, abcess or sloughing may be expected; and a tendency to visceral protrusion must be afterwards guarded against.

-Penetrating Wounds: A penetrating wound of the abdomen, whether the viscera be wounded or not, is usually attended with a great amount of "shock". The prognosis will be extremely unfavorable, if there is reason to fear the projectile has lodged in the cavity of the peritoneum...The liability to accumulation of blood in the cavity, from some vessel of the abdominal wall being involved in the wound, must not be forgotten. When, in addition to the cavity being opened, viscera are penetrated, and death does not directly ensue from rupture of some of the larger arteries, the shock is not only very severe, but the collapse attending it is seldom recovered from up to the time of the fatal termination of the case.

If the stomach has been penetrated, there will probably be vomiting of blood from the first. If the liver or spleen be wounded, death from hemorrhage is likely to follow quickly. If the small intestines have been perforated, and death follows soon after from peritonitis, the bowels usually remain unmoved, so that no evidence is offered of the nature of the wound from evacuations. If the kidneys or bladder are penetrated, the escape of urine into the abdomen is almost a certain cause of fatal result. Gunshot wounds of the colon, especially of the sigmoid flexure, appear to be less fatal than wounds of the small intestine.

When the abdominal parietes have been opened...protrusion of omentum and intestines will probably be one of the results.

-Treatment: In the general treatment of penetrating wounds of the abdomen by gunshot, the surgeon can do little more than to soothe and relieve the patient by the administration of opiates, and to treat symptoms of inflammation when they arise on the same principles as in all other cases. The collapse which attends such injuries may be useful in checking hemorrhage. If the intestine protrudes...it must be returned. If the intestine be wounded, sutures are inapplicable without previously removing the contused edges.

In 1861, J. Julian Chisolm, M.D. wrote "*A Manual of Military Surgery.*" Dr. Chisolm was Professor of Surgery at the Medical College of the State of South Carolina. His text was written specifically for use by Confederate Army surgeons. The manual contains these instructions and caveats: "Never probe perforating wounds of the abdomen, and, especially, never attempt to search for foreign bodies which have passed beyond the abdominal walls; Sew up intestinal wounds; Dilate wound in abdomen when necessary to relieve strangulation and facilitate reduction; Where the larger viscera are injured, recovery is rare; Avoid using purgatives when the intestine is wounded; Peritonitis is a common cause of mortality; Where the intestine is much crushed, leave it out of the wound, or excise the crushed portion and close the intestinal wound by sutures; In wounds of the bladder, continued use of catheter essential."[104]

The overall mortality for abdominal wounds was 87%. If the peritoneum alone was penetrated, mortality was 25%. Penetration of the large intestine resulted in a mortality rate of 59%. Trauma to the liver, spleen, stomach, small intestine, or kidneys resulted in near 100% mortality. Trauma to the pelvis, with bony injury, or trauma to the bladder or rectum, resulted in mortality rates of 80%.[105]

The basic treatment for penetrating injuries was to push any protruding intestines back into the abdominal cavity and place a dressing over the hole. Fever and inflammation were treated later as necessary. Surgeons, as well as soldiers, considered serious abdominal wounds mortal. On the battlefield, wounded soldiers often pulled open their shirts looking for abdominal wounds. Due to the tremendous number of casualties that presented to a field hospital during a battle, soldiers with serious abdominal wounds were often made as comfortable as possible, given narcotics and water, and allowed to die. In the rare event that a soldier survived, he was treated for complications as they arose, usually after transfer to a general hospital.

Union soldier Andrew Roy was wounded at the Battle of Gaine's Mill, in 1862. He wrote the following letter:

> My Dear Mother - Three days ago I was wounded in the left side, the
> ball passing through my body just above the groin, in a bayonet charge
> at the battle of Gaine's Mill, and the wound is probably mortal.
> I am a prisoner of war, and am left with many others on the battle-
> field. I will keep this letter in my blouse pocket, and if I die it will be
> sent to you by some of my comrades after they are exchanged.
> Dear mother, farewell,
> Your loving son,
> Andrew Roy

Fortunately, Roy was one of the lucky ones. He survived his wounds and died in 1914, at the age of eighty.[106]

MISCELLANEOUS SURGICAL CONCEPTS:

Hemorrhagic Shock:

Civil War physicians had no understanding of the modern concept of hemorrhagic shock. Hemorrhagic shock is defined as the decreased perfusion of vital organs, secondary to the loss of blood. As blood volume decreases, blood pressure drops, and vital organs such as the brain, heart, and kidneys sustain irreparable damage, due to a lack of blood flow. If blood loss reaches a critical point, death occurs.

Civil War surgeons did take note of shock symptoms and signs; anxiety, restlessness, confusion, pallor, cool and clammy skin, and a weak pulse. Shock was felt to be a "sudden prostration of the vital powers due to injury or emotion."[107] It was often referred to as "nervous shock". The standard treatment for shock was a "stimulant" dose of alcohol. As Dr. Smith states, "if shock exists, the administration of a little wine, aromatic ammonia, or other restorative, in water, may prove of great service to the patient."[108] Whiskey was the "stimulant" most often used. The term "collapse" was used to refer to profound, and generally terminal shock, with loss of consciousness and, eventually, vital signs.

Many surgeons believed that shock was a good thing. The belief was that, as blood volume decreased, blood flow from a wound slowed. The slow flowing blood could then clot, stopping further bleeding, and potentially saving the life of the soldier. As Chisolm wrote, "...In nervous shock, with the suspension in the circulatory function, lies the safety of many a wounded soldier....little blood escapes from the injured vessels, and there is no force from behind, owing to the diminished action of the heart, to drive on and keep in motion this blood, so its clotting is favored....the formation of a clot plugs up the orifice in a bleeding vessel, and stops any further loss of blood."[109]

Amazingly, several 1861 texts suggest the use of systemic blood-letting to arrest uncontrollable hemorrhage from gunshot wounds. In his section on abdominal trauma, Chisolm states, "...if nervous shock is not present, the patient should be bled nearly to syncope for its anti-hemorrhagic effect."[110] Writing about the control of hemorrhaging from the chest, Smith recommends, "...if the patient be sufficiently strong, bleeding from a large opening until syncope supervenes."[111] Obviously, this method of treatment makes no sense whatsoever. While it is true that as one purposely bleeds an injured soldier from a surgically incised vein, the bleeding will eventually stop at the site of an injury, the ultimate result is the same; hemorrhagic shock. That medical minds of the day even considered this form of treatment is hard to comprehend. One advantage of the large numbers of casualties Civil War surgeons had to attend to was that they observed the results of their treatments time and time again. It did not take long to see that bleeding an injured soldier did little to help him, and no doubt many a soldier died while the surgeon was performing the task. Therefore, systemic blood-letting rapidly fell out of favor, and was seldom recommended, or practiced, shortly after the start of the war.

Hemorrhage:

Obviously, the control of bleeding was a primary concern of Civil War surgeons. Surgeons divided hemorrhage into two classes. "Primary hemorrhage" was bleeding that occurred from the time of injury to within twenty-four hours of the injury. It was due to bleeding from traumatized blood vessels. "Secondary hemorrhage" occurred after the first twenty-four hours, often six to ten days after the initial injury. Secondary hemorrhages usually occurred at surgical sites, and were related to ligatures being removed from major blood vessels, either manually or spontaneously.

Primary hemorrhage was treated in a number of ways, including direct pressure, tourniquets, ligature, and styptics. Initially, direct pressure would be applied to the wound with a wad of lint, or a pad of linen or cotton cloth. The compressive pad was held in place manually or a roller-dressing could be applied. Most bleeding could be controlled in this fashion.

In cases of massive hemorrhage from major arteries, tourniquets were used. Tourniquets were applied proximal to the wound and tightened until the bleeding stopped. Tourniquets used included the "Spanish Windlass", made by tying a length of cloth around the limb, inserting a stick between the skin and the cloth, and turning the stick to twist the cloth tight enough to control bleeding. The field tourniquet was a cloth belt with a metal buckle that could clamp onto the belt at any position. The belt was pulled tight manually and the buckle fastened to hold it in place. Various buckle mechanisms were available; all using the same principle. Most surgical sets contained one or more Petit tourniquets. Petit tourniquets consisted of a belt to wrap around the limb and a mechanical device that included a screw mechanism that would tighten the belt. Whichever tourniquet was used the end result was the same; interruption of arterial blood flow to the affected limb.

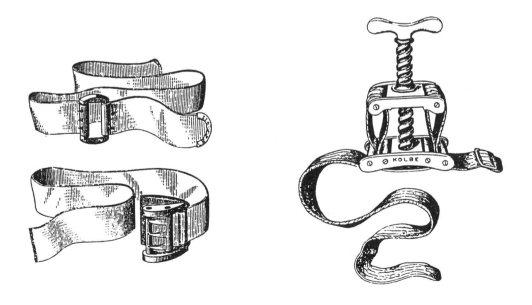

Figure 12: The field tourniquet (left) and the Petit tourniquet

Many of these tourniquets were applied at battlefield dressing stations, or upon arrival to a field hospital. Surgical procedures were occasionally delayed for several hours, depending on the number of casualties at the facility. The complete disruption of arterial blood flow to a limb, for a period of hours, resulted in irreversible ischemic damage. Certainly, many limbs that might have been salvageable were lost, due to the injudicious or prolonged use of these tourniquets.

As described above, since patients who hemorrhaged to the point of syncope (fainting) often stopped bleeding from their wounds, some surgeons would wait until the soldier became unconscious before applying a tourniquet. A practice doomed to cause more harm than good.

Another method used to control bleeding was direct ligature of a bleeding vessel. Using this technique, individual arteries, and occasionally large veins, were tied off using a variety of materials. The materials used for ligatures included cat-gut, deer sinew, thread made of cotton, linen, or silk, or metallic wire made of gold, silver, iron, or lead. "Saddler's silk" was the most popular material used during the war.

Ligature is a very precise and effective way to arrest blood loss. However, this could be technically difficult, time consuming, and often led to serious complications. To ligate an artery, it had to be exposed at a site proximal to the wound in order to get a tie around it. This exposure was accomplished by incising the skin, dissecting down to the vessel, grasping the artery with arterial forceps, lifting the vessel, and placing a silk tie around it. The tie was passed under the artery, either with a finger tip, or with the aid of various types of guides or directors. After the tie was looped around the vessel, it was firmly tightened and knotted to stop distal blood flow.

In the case of amputation stumps, surgically transected arteries were grasped with a forceps, or an instrument called a tenaculum. A tenaculum was a long, curved hook which could pierce the wall of a transected artery in order to pull it out of the stump. A tie could then be placed around the exposed artery. When the tenaculum was removed, the artery retracted back into the stump with the tie attached.

Civil War surgeons recognized that foreign material left in a wound led to severe inflammation, which slowed or prevented healing. Therefore, the practice of the day was to remove sutures and ties, after they felt the vessels had healed. When an artery was tied, one end of the silk tie was left long and protruding from the incision. The surgeon would then gently tug on the ligature each day until the tie came free and could be pulled from the wound. The tie often separated between the sixth and tenth day after the operation. In many instances, this led to significant bleeding - known as secondary hemorrhage. Some secondary hemorrhages were caused by the natural breakdown of blood clots in and around large blood vessels, but the majority were the result of the surgeon pulling the ligature off a previously ligated vessel. In his discussion of secondary hemorrhage in "*The Hand-Book of Surgical Operations,*" Dr. Smith also notes that secondary bleeding "may be excited by stimulus of any kind, such as venereal excitement or excess in drinking."[112] Treatment options included pressure dressings, attempts to re-tie the vessel, or styptics. The mortality rate of secondary hemorrhage was about 60%.[113]

Cases of relatively minor bleeding could occasionally be controlled by using styptics. These chemicals cauterized tissue, and could be used to chemically sear the bleeding vessel. To be effective, the bleeding had to be fairly slow and of low volume, so as not to flush the chemical away. Styptics were available in solid or solution form.

Commonly used compounds included persulfate of iron - known as Monsel's salt, alum, copper sulfate, and silver nitrate. The number of cases of significant bleeding that could be controlled by cautery was very small, but they were occasionally useful in the treatment of minor, but persistent, bleeding.

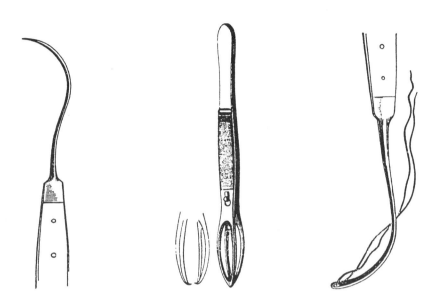

Figure 13: Instruments used to ligate vessels.
A tenaculum, an arterial forceps, and an aneurysm needle - used to guide a tie around a vessel

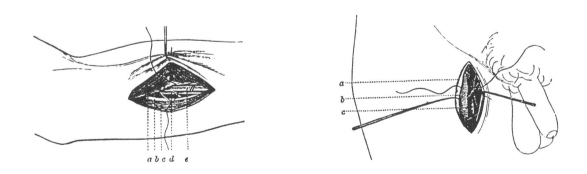

Figure 14: Diagrams of surgical "cut-downs" used to obtain access to arteries.
Forearm (left) and groin

Wound Closure:

Civil War surgeons were presented with countless traumatic lacerations, as well as surgical incisions that required repair. Surgeons did not understand the cause of the inflammation that occurred when non-sterile sutures were placed through the skin, but they did recognize that the inflammatory process interfered with the healing of wounds. Due to the problems inherent with introducing non-sterile material into a wound, Civil War surgeons often tried to close wounds with adhesive plaster. Adhesive plaster was made by mixing lead plaster, resin, and water, and spreading this mixture on one side of a strip of thin muslin. The strip was then allowed to dry for storage. When a surgeon wanted to use the strip, he re-moistened it with water. One end of the adhesive strip was placed on intact skin, on one side of the wound, the wound edges were held together by hand, and the other end of the strip was stretched across the laceration, and applied to the skin on the opposite side of the wound. The adhesive strip then held the wound edges together. These dressings were used to approximate the edges of traumatic lacerations, as well as surgical incisions.

If a surgeon did choose to close a wound with sutures, silk was the material most commonly used. Fine metallic wire was also used and was less likely to cause inflammation. Surgical sewing needles were made of silver or steel. They were available in a variety of sizes; straight and curved.

An interesting technique - known as the twisted suture - combined the use of less irritating metal, along with the holding property of silk. The wound edges were manually approximated and a long, straight metallic needle or pin was inserted into the skin on one side of the wound. The needle was tunneled under the skin, across the wound, and then pushed out through the skin on the opposite side. Silk suture material was then wrapped in a "figure-of-eight" fashion around the exposed head and point of the needle, pulling the wound edges together and holding the needle in place. A series of these needles were placed along the entire length of the wound. Figure-of-eight wraps were then done from needle to needle to stabilize the repair.

Figure 15: The "figure-of eight" or twisted suture

Confederate surgeons occasionally ran out of silk suture and used horse hair instead. Since horse hair is stiff and difficult to work with, it was boiled to render it soft and pliant. The hair was inadvertently cleaned and sterilized in the process. Confederate surgeons noted that wounds sutured with this horse hair developed inflammation less often.[114]

Serrefines were small, spring-loaded clips that could be used to pinch the edges of a wound together until it healed. They were used only occasionally as they were not always available.

Figure 16: A serrefine

Dressings:

Civil War surgeons, stewards, and nurses applied and changed innumerable dressings. Dressings were applied to injuries such as abrasions, lacerations, and amputation stumps. Many Civil War medical texts contained chapters devoted to the application of various types of dressings. Detailed illustrations showed precisely how the dressings were to be applied.

One of the most universally used dressing materials was lint. Lint was made by scraping old linen with a knife, or by pulling out the cross-threads from a piece of linen. Some lint was very fine, almost downy in nature, whereas some was more coarse. Lint made by machine was known as "patent lint". Lint was used primarily as a compressive-type dressing. This fluffy material was folded into compresses and stuffed into wounds to control bleeding, or placed on an amputation stump, under a cloth dressing. Clumps of lint were also wetted and used as sponges to clean wounds.

Most wounds were covered with wet compresses or "water-dressings," and there was considerable debate throughout the war, as to whether the water used should be cold or warm. Cold water dressings were most often recommended and utilized. A cold water dressing was made by soaking a piece of folded lint with cold water, the wet lint was placed in or on the wound, and the lint was held in place by a cloth wrap or adhesive plaster. The wet lint dressing would be changed at least daily and sometimes more often. These cold water dressings helped to control bleeding, but more importantly, helped keep wound inflammation in check.

Charpie was a dressing composed of the separated threads of linen or cotton fabric. The threads were clumped together to make a porous mass. The materials used to make charpie were coarser than those used to make lint. Charpie was used mainly to absorb wound drainage, and was employed in the dressing of stumps, abscesses, and purulent wounds.

Cotton, muslin, flannel, linen, and other materials were available in rolls of various size and thickness. These materials were used to pad splints, wrap amputation stumps, and dress abrasions, lacerations, and burns. Occasionally, an elastic material know as "gum elastic cloth" was also used.

Amputation stumps were often dressed with adhesive plaster. This dressing would adhere to the skin and could remain in place for quite some time. The dressing would stay in place until the strips were once again softened by moistening them with water. Isenglass plaster was a commercially available adhesive plaster. It was less irritating to the skin than standard adhesive plaster, but more expensive and harder to come by.

In "*The Hospital Steward's Manual*", Woodward describes the dressing box and some of its contents:

> A shallow box should be made, two feet long by eighteen inches wide and four inches deep, divided into equal halves by a partition which rises in the center to a height of eight inches, and has an opening cut in it in such a manner as to serve for a handle. In this box should be placed the following articles:
>
>   Patent lint, neatly rolled; some charpie, or packed lint; an assortment of roller-bandages of various widths; adhesive plaster cut into strips three-fourths of an inch wide, also a roll of uncut; isenglass plaster; two bundles of ligatures ten inches long, composed each of a single thickness of saddler's silk well waxed, and one of the ligatures of two thicknesses twisted together, each bundle consisting of at least a dozen ligatures laid side by side, and surrounded for about half their length by a roll of paper fastened by a pin, so that the ligatures may be drawn out one at a time as wanted; a large pair of scissors; a sheet of patent lint eighteen inches square, neatly spread on one side with simple cerate; a pincushion amply provided with pins at one end, with from three to a dozen surgical needles ready-threaded at the other; a pocket set of instruments; three to a dozen towels; and some sponges.[115]

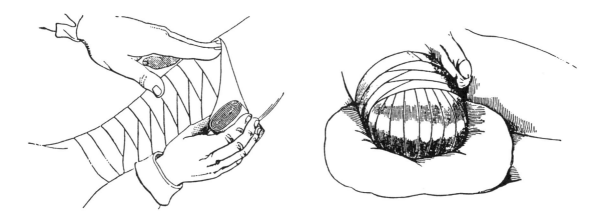

Figure 17: Dressing illustrations

Disinfectants:

To say that Civil War surgeons knew nothing of infection is, without doubt, a true statement. To say that they were not concerned about its resultant inflammation, is not. Civil War wounds, whether traumatic or surgical, almost universally became infected. As previously discussed, the total lack of aseptic surgical technique and treatment was to blame. Surgeons had no concept of the microbial nature of infection. They believed that post-operative inflammation resulted from natural healing processes gone awry, or was due to extrinsic environmental factors. Surgeons anticipated the discharge of purulent material from a wound a few days after surgery. They believed this pus to be the slough of dead, necrotic tissue from the wound; a sign of a healthy healing process. This initial purulent drainage was referred to as "laudable pus." Apparently, the immune systems of many soldiers were able to combat infection at this early stage, and the inflammation eventually subsided, so that healing did occur. However, if the infection progressed, inflammation gradually worsened. The affected area became painful, hot, red, and swollen. Sometimes the entire limb became involved. Purulent drainage increased. The patient developed systemic symptoms of fever, chills, nausea, and vomiting. As bacteria gained entrance to the blood stream, the patient would become increasingly weak and lethargic, eventually lapsing into coma and probable death.

Surgeons witnessed this progression time and time again. Theories abounded as to the cause of this progressive inflammation. Most physicians blamed noxious elements in the air. Some believed that foul smells were to blame. Some came close to the truth by blaming "organic particles or fomites floating in the air."[116] Surgeons and their staffs took great care in providing adequate ventilation to hospital wards in an attempt to prevent this inflammatory process.

Eventually, surgeons began to take steps to try to stop the inflammatory process after the phase of "laudable pus". Often, cold compresses or ice were applied to the site.

By trial and error, several chemicals were applied to inflamed wounds that actually possessed disinfectant properties. "*A Manual of Minor Surgery*," written by Dr. John H. Packard in 1863, contains a chapter on disinfectants.[117] Due to the accepted theory of the day - that inflammation was caused by airborne elements - these disinfectants were usually placed in open containers on the ward, or near a patient's bed, where they could evaporate and circulate through the air. Popular disinfectants included chlorine (or chloride of lime), bromine, and carbon powder. Odorous basins, buckets, and jars were cleaned with these chemicals. Mixtures containing manganese, sulfuric acid, zinc chloride, and iodine were also used. At some point, dressings saturated with some of these chemicals began to be applied to infected wounds, resulting in decreased inflammation and improved healing. Dilute solutions of silver nitrate, nitric acid, sodium hypochlorite, permanganate of potash, lime-water, chlorine, and bromine were used in this fashion. Carbolic acid, which would later become famous as the antiseptic used by Joseph Lister, was also used by Civil War surgeons.

Unfortunately, throughout most of the war, disinfectants were used primarily as cleaning agents or air "purifiers." Only near the end of the war were they beginning to be applied to the infected wounds themselves. One theory suggests that surgeons and hospital staff noted that after they had rinsed dressing material in disinfectant solutions, cuts and abrasions on their own hands became less inflamed and healed faster. As a result of this observation, they began applying these disinfectants to the soldiers' wounds. Whatever the reason, antiseptic wound care had its beginning toward the end of the war.

Surgical Infections:

During the post-operative period, wound infection was the leading cause of morbidity and mortality. Of the soldiers who died of their wounds, approximately 61% died on the battlefield or immediately thereafter; approximately 39% died later, from secondary hemorrhage or infection. Civil War physicians feared the four surgical fevers; tetanus, erysipelas, hospital gangrene, and pyemia. Civil war surgeons recognized these diseases but never determined their causes.

Tetanus is now known to be caused by a toxin produced under anaerobic (airless) conditions by a bacterium called *Clostridium tetani*. The toxin is known as tetanospasmin, in reference to its ability to cause violent muscle spasms and generalized muscle rigidity. Tetanus is also known by the common name of "lockjaw." When the bacterium - which is common in soil - is introduced deeply into a wound, particularly puncture wounds or crush injuries, it begins producing the toxin. The toxin is carried via the bloodstream to the central nervous system and causes the characteristic symptoms. At the time of the Civil War, tetanus was ultimately fatal.

Civil War surgeons believed tetanus was caused by environmental factors such as exposure to excessive heat or cold, night air and drafts, neglect of thorough and early cleansing of a wound (actually, in part, correct), pressure upon nerves by projectiles, bone splinters or bandages, or injury to nerves when the surgeon probed or operated.[118]

Recommended treatment included the use of dressings over the wound, large doses of brandy and opium, and "the most nutritious and bracing food, through a tube introduced by the nostrils into the stomach, or by enema, as the circumstances or necessities of the case may dictate."[119]

Erysipelas is a highly contagious streptococcal infection. The usual causative organism is *Streptococcus pyogenes*. The infection causes a characteristic bright red rash. As the disease progresses, fever develops, and the patient succumbs to the toxic effects of bacteremia (bacteria in the bloodstream). It was communicated from patient to patient by dirty instruments, dressings, and the hands of doctors, nurses, and stewards. The disease tended to run in epidemics; through a ward or an entire hospital. Once the infection was present on a ward, it spread rapidly to all patients; even those without wounds.

Treatment included laxatives and diaphoretics. Occasionally, strong cathartics were used for "purging." Areas of infection around a wound were cleaned with diluted bromine or chlorine in water. Quinine was used in an attempt to relieve fever.

Interestingly, erysipelas was the disease that started surgeons thinking about the potential contagious nature of disease. They noted that if a soldier with erysipelas was placed on a ward, soon the whole ward had it. The disease also spread to some doctors, nurses, and other hospital staff. Before long, erysipelas patients were segregated into isolated wards or tents of their own. One Louisville hospital eliminated the disease in one of those wards by spraying bromine vapor into the air.[120] The disease became less frequent as better attention was paid to wound cleaning and disinfectant use became more prevalent.

Hospital gangrene was the disease most feared by surgical patients. The exact etiology of this infection is unknown but many now believe it was caused by *Streptococcus pyogenes*, possibly in conjunction with *Staphylococcus aureus*, and/or anaerobic bacteria. The disease presented as a small, black spot on a healing wound. The discoloration would spread, often to the entire limb. The central, initial spot would begin to necrose and slough. The necrosis would spread until "the whole leg or arm was but a rotten, evil-smelling mass of dead flesh."[121]

The treatment of hospital gangrene was similar to that of erysipelas. Patients were isolated, and wards were fumigated and disinfected. Highly nourishing diets were prescribed; alcohol, opium, morphine, and quinine were administered. Disinfectants were applied to the wounds. Many patients were anesthetized with chloroform, and the infection surgically debrided and cauterized with silver nitrate. Sometimes, lint soaked in turpentine was packed into the wound.[122] Cold water dressings were standard. Some surgeons surgically removed dead tissue as the disease progressed. Amputation was often required.

A serious outbreak of hospital gangrene occurred in Memphis, in 1863. Union Surgeon Middleton Goldsmith experimented with the topical application of bromine in the treatment of the infections. His results were described as "miraculous." Bromine treatment for hospital gangrene was henceforth recommended by the Medical Department and the U.S. Sanitary Commission. Also, at Memphis, a new standard was born, in that each soldier with gangrene had to have his own cup, eating utensils, and cleaning sponges.[123]

As disinfectant use became standard, the number of cases of hospital gangrene declined. It was reported, that during the last six months of its existence, there was not one case of hospital gangrene in the base hospital of the Army of the Potomac.

The treatment of hospital gangrene by Confederate surgeons was essentially the same as that employed by their Northern counterparts. In their treatment of hospital gangrene, however, Confederate surgeons occasionally relied on maggots to clean infected wounds. The fly larva would eat the dead necrotic tissue and leave the healthy tissue intact. This practice actually resulted in better wound healing.[124] Unfortunately, Union surgeons never accepted this treatment method, and, for the most part, meticulously removed maggots, either with forceps or disinfectant solutions.

Hospital gangrene was the most dreaded post-operative infection, by the soldiers, due to its disfiguring effects. Pyemia was the most dreaded infection, by the surgeons, due to its frequency and fatality rate. Pyemia literally means "pus in the blood." The infection can be caused by any bacteria that gains access to the bloodstream.

72

Pyemia occurs as bacteria spread from an infected wound site into the bloodstream. Symptoms include multiple abscesses, high fever, rapid pulse and respiration, low blood pressure, obtundation, kidney and other vital organ failure, and finally, death. Civil War statistics report the mortality rate for this infection as 97.4%.[125]

No treatment method was successful. Laxatives, cathartics, alcohol, and narcotics were administered. Since alcohol was considered a stimulant, large quantities, usually in the form of whiskey or brandy, were given.

Two other post-operative infectious conditions deserve mention.

Osteomyelitis refers to infection of bone. It occurs when an infection of the skin or soft tissues progresses into the underlying bone. The most common causative organism, in traumatic wounds, is *Staphylococcus aureus.* In acute cases, symptoms include local pain, swelling, and fever. Symptomatic treatment was similar to the above conditions. Occasionally, surgeons removed the infected bone or performed an amputation.

Unfortunately, due to the lack of aseptic surgical technique or antibiotic therapy, many Civil War patients developed chronic osteomyelitis. This deep-seated bone infection could "smolder" for years; resulting in chronic pain, fever, weakness, and weight loss. Many of these infections subsequently developed fistulous tracts to the skin, and drained purulent material for years. This chronic condition was occasionally referred to as "hectic fever," and often resulted in permanent disability.

Countless Civil war soldiers developed abscesses or "boils." These collections of pus are usually caused by *Staphylococcus aureus.* Then, as today, drainage was the mainstay of treatment. Superficial abscess were incised with a scalpel or lancet. Deep abscesses were opened surgically, or drained with a trochar and cannula. A cannula is a thin, metal tube containing a solid pointed rod (trochar) that protrudes from the end of the tube. The device is pushed into the abscess or cavity, the trochar is pulled out, and the hollow cannula is left in place. Pus then flows freely out of the cannula.

Empyema refers to a collection of pus within the chest cavity; between the lung and the ribs. This can result from pneumonia, or secondary infection after penetrating trauma. In a specialized application of the above technique, a trochar/cannula was inserted into the chest to drain these collections of pus.

Pain Control:

Pain management was a serious concern for Civil War surgeons and their patients. The use of ether and chloroform has already been discussed. Records indicate that most major surgical procedures were performed using one of these agents.

Post-operative pain control was most often accomplished by the administration of narcotics. Morphine and opium were the narcotics used.

Narcotics could be given by mouth, but often caused vomiting when given orally. In addition, the liver metabolizes a large amount of these drugs before they get into the bloodstream, so they weren't very effective by the oral route.

Narcotics (especially morphine) were available in a powdered form that could be applied directly to a fresh wound. Administered by this method, the narcotic entered the bloodstream via injured blood vessels, with greater effect.

A third route of narcotic administration was by subcutaneous injection, using a Wood's endermic syringe. Morphine (mixed with water) was the drug used. As Chisolm states in "*A Manual of Military Surgery*," "By the use of this little instrument, a new and extensive field for doing good is open to the humane military surgeon, and he who is the fortunate possessor of this talisman, will receive daily the thanks and blessings of his suffering patients."[126]

For minor surgical procedures local anesthesia was often used. Application of cold was the usual method. Regarding the application of cold, Packard describes the technique in "*A Manual of Minor Surgery*," "it is applied by means of the ordinary freezing mixture of pounded ice and salt. A sufficient quantity of this is wrapped in a piece of lint or rag, and laid over the part, which in a few minutes loses its color and temperature, and becomes hard; it may now be cut without causing any pain."[127] Procedures that could be performed under local anesthesia included the repair of small lacerations, drainage of abscesses, superficial foreign body removal, and other minor surgeries.

Fractures and Dislocations:

Civil War surgeons treated a large number of fractures and dislocations. Fractures were classified as being simple or compound. Simple fractures were broken bones that were contained within the skin. Compound fractures penetrated the skin and were much more dangerous. As Packard states, "a simple fracture, painful as it may be, is not apt to involve any danger...with compound fracture...the patient runs the risk of inflammation, suppuration, tetanus, and hectic fever."[128] Since X-rays had not yet been discovered, diagnosis was made by abnormal movement at the site, or by noting crepitus. Crepitus is the grinding and crunching sensation felt, as broken bones shift and rub together under the skin.

Treatment of fractures included alcohol stimulus or narcotics for pain relief. If the fracture was simple and in good position, the extremity was splinted with wooden or plaster splints. A special wooden "fracture box" was sometimes used on fractures of the lower leg. The "box" supported the back and sides of the lower leg as well as the foot. Fractures of the femur were treated by bedrest with traction. The shoulders were tied to the bed and weight was applied to the affected leg. Various devices and pulley arrangements supplied this inline traction. The weight applied varied from 5 to 30 lbs. depending on the size and muscular development of the patient. Constant traction, for several weeks, held the bones in place until healing occurred. One method of applying traction weight was developed by Dr. Gurdon Buck of New York. Using this method, a traction weight was attached to a strap that was wrapped around the ankle. The weight was then suspended by a pulley, producing traction in-line with the leg This technique was utilized during the war and is still used in the treatment of hip fractures today - referred to as "Buck's traction."

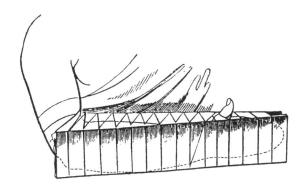

Figure 18: Double splint for forearm fracture

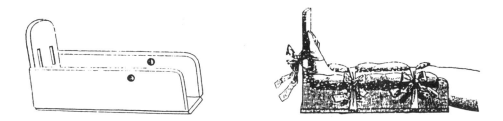

Figure 19: Fracture-box for fracture of the lower leg

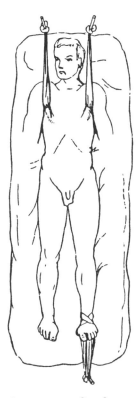

Figure 20: Traction set-up for fracture of the femur

Compound fractures could be treated conservatively, or by resection or amputation. Treatment depended on the severity of the fracture, the skill of the surgeon, and the number of casualties that required treatment. If conservative treatment was planned, the fracture was reduced (re-aligned) so the protruding bone retracted back under the skin. If fragments of bone protruded from the wound, and could not be reduced, the protruding parts were snipped away with a bone forceps or sawed off. Any pieces of loose bone were removed. Small skin lacerations were dressed with lint or cotton. Larger lacerations were usually closed with adhesive plaster. Bran or sawdust was sometimes heaped over an open fracture site to keep the area clean, and prevent flies from laying eggs in the wound.

After the fracture was reduced, and the wound repaired or dressed, the limb was splinted or placed in traction as described above.

Compound fractures, treated conservatively, often became infected. Packard states, "during the first few days, fever will be apt to occur, and must be subdued by low diet, cooling drinks, and the avoidance of noise or excitement."[129]

Compound fractures were prone to develop hospital gangrene and later require amputation. They also could heal with a non-union of the bone, resulting in a pseudoarthrosis - or false joint. A non-union required continuous splinting or special braces to maintain the function of the limb. Sometimes, this was more cumbersome and difficult to manage than an amputation with a prosthesis would have been.

A Civil War surgeon also required skill in managing joint dislocations. The hallmarks of this diagnosis were pain, deformity, and impairment of motion at a joint. Occasionally, shortening (rarely lengthening) of the affected part was noted as well. Diagnosis and reduction of dislocations required knowledge of joint anatomy. Most dislocations were reduced by gentle, but forceful, traction, to reduce any over-riding of the joint surfaces, and manipulation of the displaced part back into position.

Small joints, such as fingers or toes, were reduced without anesthesia, or perhaps after the administration of a narcotic. Large joints such as the shoulder, elbow, wrist, hip, knee, or ankle were reduced after the patient was anesthetized with ether or chloroform.

Other Procedures:

Civil War surgeons were called upon to remove countless foreign bodies from the skin and eyes. Small or superficial foreign bodies in the skin could often be removed with a needle. Large and deep foreign bodies were removed with a scalpel and forceps. If a foreign body was felt to be inaccessible, it was left in place. Many of these healed fine, with no further problems. Others became badly infected, causing serious illness or death. Occasionally, attempts were made to surgically remove these, weeks or even months after the injury. Some retained foreign bodies gradually worked themselves to the surface many years after the injury.

Foreign bodies in the eye could be very serious. Superficial foreign bodies were removed with a needle or the pointed tip of a scalpel. Foreign bodies that penetrated the globe often resulted in severe infection, and the loss of site in that eye. Eye infections were treated with rest and cold compresses, with generally poor results.

U.S. surgeons performed the majority of dental work on Union soldiers. In the South, dental work was generally performed by dentists. Dentists were drafted by the Confederate government and given the same rank and pay as hospital stewards. Dental work primarily consisted of "filling and extracting teeth, removing tartar, adjusting fractures of the bones of the mouth, and treating wounds of the face."[130]

Dr. James Baxter Bean, an Atlanta dentist, developed an interdental splint which he used in the treatment of maxillary fractures. His success with these types of fractures was phenomenal. Many Confederate soldiers with maxillary fractures were sent to Atlanta to be treated by Dr. Bean. Confederate Surgeon General Moore ordered all general hospitals to obtain these devices, and Bean himself provided instruction on their use to the surgeons-in-charge. It is believed that the military hospital in Atlanta was the first in military or dental history to be used for maxillo-facial surgery.[131]

Seriously ill or injured soldiers were often unable to void when necessary. In addition, some of the medications they were given could cause urinary retention. Trauma to the central nervous system resulted in an inability to void, as did trauma to the abdomen and pelvis.

Most Civil War surgical sets, including pocket kits, contained urinary catheters. Most of these were made of silver or another metal. Gum-elastic catheters were also available.

Catheters were inserted when bladder distention was noted by the patient or the surgeon. Usually, the urine would be drained and the catheter removed. Occassionally, the catheter would be left in place for continual drainage. Catheters had a small ring at the distal end, to which cords could be attached and tied around the patient, to hold the catheter in place.

Figure 21: Urinary catheter

III - CIVIL WAR MEDICINE:

<u>The Diseases:</u>

   Civil War doctors were not only surgeons but medical practitioners as well. In the 1860's, physicians were not separated by specialty; each took care of surgical and medical cases. As already noted, two-thirds of the fatalities of the Civil War died from disease. These statistics do not include fatal infections resulting from battle wounds. It has been estimated that Union surgeons treated 6,000,000 cases of illness as compared to 400,000 war wounds.[132] Confederate Medical Inspector, Dr. Joseph Jones, estimated that each Confederate soldier was sick an average of six times.[133] Regimental surgeons and their assistants were presented with dozens of ill soldiers at daily sick call. General hospital wards contained hundreds of medically ill soldiers. If the stereotypical Civil War doctor is pictured as a surgeon - blood up to his elbows, sawing off another limb - it is because of the uniqueness of that aspect of military medicine. For shear caseload, the Civil War doctor was a man of medical practice.
   The diseases that brought soldiers to the attention of the Civil War physician were basically the same ones he had dealt with in civilian practice; the main difference was in the numbers. Civil War soldiers were housed in crowded camps and infectious diseases ran rampant. Many soldiers had led relatively isolated rural lives and were now grouped together with large numbers of men for the first time. Many were exposed to illnesses for which they had developed no prior immunity. Poor camp hygiene allowed soldiers to be exposed to fecally contaminated food and water. There were many times when the majority of soldiers in any given regiment was ill.

   Medical theory at the time of the Civil War did not include any concept of the microbial nature of illness. In 1863, Dr. J.J. Woodward wrote "*Outlines of the Chief Camp Diseases of the United States Army*," conforming to the accepted medical theories of the day.[134] The purpose of his text was to familiarize the Civil War physician with the illnesses that were common to soldiers in camp.
   In his book, he discussed the Zymotic Diseases, defined as those which are epidemic, endemic, or communicable. He separated these illnesses into three main categories -
   The first, and largest, category included the Miasmatic Diseases. Miasms were thought to be noxious substances in the air that led to disease. Miasms were further subdivided into koinomiasmata, which arose from decomposing vegetable matter, and idiomiasmata, which arose by "decomposition of matters derived from the human body." Terms in common usage included the "malarial miasms" of swamps, the "mephitic effluvia" of latrines or rotting garbage, and "crowd poisoning", which occurred when men slept in crowded, stuffy tents.
   The Miasmatic Diseases were:
> Typhoid fever
> Typhus fever
> Typho-malarial fever
> Yellow fever
> Remittent fever (malaria)

Intermittent fever (malaria); sub-divided:
  -Quotidian
  -Tertian
  -Quartan
  -Congestive
Diarrhea; sub-divided:
  -Acute
  -Chronic
Dysentery; sub-divided:
  -Acute
  -Chronic
Epidemic cholera
Erysipelas
Hospital gangrene
Pyemia
Smallpox
Varioloid (a mild form of smallpox)
Measles
Scarlet fever
Diptheria
Mumps
Epidemic catarrh (common cold)
(modern terms in parentheses)

The second category of camp diseases included the Enthetic Diseases. The term enthetic comes from the Greek word for implanted. This category included diseases that were "inoculated." The Enthetic Diseases were:

Syphilis
Gonorrhea
Gonorrheal orchitis (gonorrheal testicular infection)
Stricture of the urethra
Purulent opthalmia (gonorrheal conjunctivitis or eye infection)
Hydrophobia (rabies)
Glanders (a nasal infection of animals; spread to man, usually by horses)
Bites of serpents
Other diseases of this order
(modern terms in parentheses)

The third category of camp diseases included the Dietic Diseases. These diseases were related to diet. The category included:

Starvation
Scurvy
Purpura (easy bruisability due to Vitamin K deficiency,
resulted from the absence of green vegetables in the diet)
Inebriation (alcohol intoxication)
Delerium tremens (alcohol withdrawl symptoms)

Chronic alcoholism
Other diseases of this order
(modern terms in parentheses)

- *"The Medical and Surgical History of the War of the Rebellion"* lists diseases under the following classes:[135]

    Class 1. Zymotic diseases
        Order1. Miasmatic
        Order2. Enthetic
        Order3. Dietic

    Class 2. Constitutional Diseases
        Order 1. Diathetic (diseases such as gout and rheumatism)
        Order 2. Tubercular (tuberculosis)

    Class 3. Parasitic Diseases

    Class 4. Local Disease
        Order 1. Nervous system
        Order 2. Eye
        Order 3. Ear
        Order 4. Organs of Circulation
        Order 5. Respiratory Organs
        Order 6. Digestive Organs
        Order 7. Urinary and Genital Organs
        Order 8. Bones and Joints
        Order 9. Integumentary

    Class 5. Wounds, Accidents, and Injuries
        Order 1. Wounds, accidents, and injuries
        Order 2. Homicide
        Order 3. Suicide
        Order 4. Execution

- Confederate medical regulations listed a total of 130 diseases under the following main headings:[136]

        Fevers
        Diseases of the organs connected with the digestive system
        Diseases of the respiratory system
        Diseases of the circulatory system
        Diseases of the brain and nervous system
        Diseases of the urinary and genital organs and venereal affections
        Diseases of the serous exhalent vessels

Diseases of the fibrous and muscular structures
Abscesses and ulcers
Diseases of the eye
Diseases of the ear
All other diseases

Regardless of the classification scheme used, the Zymotic Diseases were the ones of the most significance, in terms of overall morbidity and mortality, to the Civil War physician and soldier. Woodward recognized that in the first year of the war, two-thirds of the diseases diagnosed in ill soldiers fell into this catagory. In his own words, "Zymotic diseases are wide-spread constitutional affections produced among masses of men by ill-understood causes, which modify profoundly the normal condition of the whole system."[137]

Dr. John Chisolm, one of the greatest medical minds of the South, stated, "continued exposure and fatigue, bad and insufficient food, salt meat, indifferent clothing, want of cleanliness, poor shelter, exposure at night to sudden changes of temperature, infected tents and camps, form a combination of causes which explains the fatality of an army in the field."[138]

Dr. Charles Tripler, author of a premier military medical text and Medical Director of the Army of the Potomac, stated, "to bad cooking, bad police, bad ventilation of tents, inattention to personal cleanliness, and unnecessarily irregular habits we are to attribute the greater proportion of the diseases that actually occured in the army."[139]

We now know that the majority of "Zymotic Diseases" are infectious illnesses; spread by specific microbial organisms, including various bacterial, parasitic, and viral pathogens.

Many factors combined to produce the phenomenal number of cases of illness found in both armies.

One source of infectious illness was via the enlistment of new recruits. Doctors were responsible for the inspection and examination of new soldiers. It was their responsibility to weed out ill and disabled recruits. The examination was to consist of a thorough assessment in order to diagnose acute or chronic problems. The examining physician was to ask specific questions such as, "Have you ever been sick?" - "When and of what diseases?" - "Have you any disease now?" - etc.[140] The recruit then stripped and received a complete physical exam. If the physician found any evidence of acute illness, or chronic disability from previous illness or injury, the recruit was supposed to be disqualified from duty.

Unfortunately, the ideal was not often practiced. Both sides in the conflict required large numbers of soldiers; quotas had to be met. Unfit volunteers frequently passed inspection. Some had no examination at all, or a very cursory one. Obvious cases of illness and disability were ignored. While some physicians took this aspect of their job seriously, others felt the task demeaning and superfluous. There were several reports of large groups of soldiers being declared fit for duty, as they were paraded past the regimental surgeon - if they could march, they could fight.

The result of this lax inspection process was that ill soldiers were placed among the ranks in crowded, unsanitary conditions.

A second factor allowing for the presence and spread of disease was the near universal lack of proper camp hygiene.

At the time of the Civil War, many physicians had great concern over maintaining a clean camp. Due to their concern over the presence of "miasmas" and "effluvia" (foul odors), they became worried if the camps developed a foul smell. Dr. Hamilton stated, "Filth and dirt become more active destroyers of life when they cooperate with pestilential states of atmosphere, or insalubrious gases, the production of unhealthy climates, or noxious situations. Cleanliness should be enforced upon soldiers with the most rigid laws."[141]

Early in the war, the U.S. Sanitary Commission produced several pamphlets concerning the subject of camp hygiene. Unfortunately, officers, as well the rank and file, seem to have shown little concern over hygienic principles. Whether out of ignorance or laziness, camp hygiene was largely ignored. Latrines were often dug shallow, allowed to overflow, and were commonly located near camp water supplies. As a result, water supplies frequently became contaminated by human waste. At night, soldiers often relieved themselves just outside their tents. Bathing was a rare occurrence and often took place in contaminated water. As a result, diarrhea became a near universal ailment. However, most officers, and many surgeons, blamed outbreaks of diarrhea on bad food or improper diet. Woodward himself blamed "the indiscreet use of unripe or uncooked vegetables" or "a sudden supply of sutler's wares, such as pies, cakes, spruce beer, and the like." He cited other factors such as "the action of saline drinking water, and exposures to heat and cold, particularly such exposure as results from sleeping on the damp ground at night."[142] It appears that no one associated fecal contamination of food or water with the occurrence of outbreaks of diarrhea. Today we know these particular illnesses are caused by fecal contamination of food and water by a variety of microorganisms. These microorganisms include bacteria such as *E. coli*, *Salmonella*, and *Shigella*, parasites such as *Giardia lambia* and *Entamoeba hystolytica* (amebic dysentery), and several viruses. Fortunately, Civil War officers gradually realized that soldiers who were quartered in clean camps, that adhered to recommended hygienic principles, were healthier and had a lower incidence of diarrheal illness. General Order No. 52, issued in May, 1863, for the Army of the Potomac, outlined mandatory sanitary practice. Camps were to be drained by a series of ditches eighteen inches deep; tents were to be struck twice a week to allow the sunning of floors and their contents; cooking was to be done by company cooks; all refuse was to be burned or buried daily; latrines were to be eight feet deep, on which six inches of dirt was to be shoveled each evening. Personal hygiene was regulated by requirements that the men wear their hair cut short, bathe twice a week, and change their clothing at least once a week.[143] Adherence to these regulations certainly was not universal, but gradual improvement was made throughout the war.

Diarrhea was the illness most commonly treated by Union and Confederate doctors. Of all the illnesses, it killed the most soldiers. Diarrheal illnesses were separated into four categories; acute diarrhea, chronic diarrhea, acute dysentery, and chronic dysentery. The diarrheas/dysenteries were also referred to as "fluxes." In many cases, these illnesses were probably different points on the spectrum of the same basic disease. Also, various microbes were most likely involved, including viruses, bacteria, and parasites; each giving rise to somewhat different symptoms. The "diarrheas" produced loose, watery stools and low grade fever. The "dysenteries" produced bloody stools and higher fevers. The acute conditions struck suddenly, producing severe symptoms of diarrhea, bloody stools, and fever. The chronic conditions were more prolonged and symptoms more low-grade, producing generalized weakness and wasting. Some soldiers who developed bouts of recurrent diarrhea were diagnosed as chronic cases, when they may simply have been exposed to different infectious organisms. Certainly, there was considerable overlap among these illnesses.

The incidence of diarrheal illness is reflected in the following statistics. In the first two years of the war, Confederate doctors treated a total of 848,555 individual cases of illness; 226,828 (27 %) were diagnosed with diarrhea or dysentery. In a series of 50,350 soldiers admitted to Chimborazo Hospital in Richmond, 10,503 (21%) had one of these diagnoses.[144] Union statistics for the entire war reveal 1,585,236 cases of diarrhea or dysentery. Of these, 1,155,266 cases were diagnosed with acute diarrhea. Diarrheal illnesses resulted in 37,794 Union deaths; the largest single cause of death due to the various diseases suffered by the soldiers.[145]

The second leading cause of death was typhoid fever. It resulted in 27,050 Union deaths out of 75,368 reported cases. Typhoid fever, and the less prevalent typhus (or typhus fever), were listed among the so-called "continued fevers", due to their propensity to cause continued, unremitting fever. Woodward's text places these illnesses in a chapter entitled "Crowd Poisoning." These illnesses were felt to be caused by exposure to noxious substances found in the air, under close and crowded conditions. He states, "the air of crowded cities, camps, and habitations becomes contaminated through effluvia from the skin and by the decomposition of the various normal and abnormal excreta. ...also the consumption of atmospheric oxygen and the substitution of carbolic acid in the ordinary process of respiration may take place to such an extent as even to induce fatal results."[146]

Typhoid fever is now known to be caused by the bacterium *Salmonella typhi*. As with the other diarrheal illnesses discussed above, it is transmitted primarily by fecally contaminated food and water. Symptoms include a continuous rising fever, fatigue, mental depression, a rose-colored rash on the chest and abdomen, diarrhea, and occasionally, bloody stools.

Typhus is an illness caused by the bacterium *Rickettsia prowazekii*. In its epidemic form, it is spread by body lice. The disease is marked by a continuous high fever, headache, myalgias, physical and mental depression, constipation, and a pink to red truncal rash. Union doctors recorded 2,504 such cases. The disease resulted in 850 deaths.

Common continual fever was an illness characterized by unremitting fever, headache, physical and mental depression, diarrhea or constipation, and absence of a rash. There was probably no one specific etiology for this constellation of symptoms, and the illness could have been caused by a variety of microbial pathogens. Also, less severe or "atypical" cases of the above mentioned "continued fevers" could have been the cause. Union statistics list 11,898 total cases; 147 fatalities.

Malarial fevers were second only to the diarrhea-dysentery illnesses in terms of overall frequency. These were known as "intermittent fevers" due to their characteristic periods of high fever and chills, followed by periods of normal temperature, or "remittent fevers" if the temperature did not return completely to normal between paroxysms. The paroxysms of fever would recur at regular intervals that determined the classification of the illness. Quotidian fever produced a daily fever spike. Tertian fever produced a fever every other day (day one was the first day of fever; day two was characterized by a normal temperature; day three the fever returned - hence the term "tertian fever"). Quartan fever produced a fever every third day. Congestive (or pernicious) intermittent fever was an unusually severe, and often fatal form, of any of the above intermittent fevers.

The term malaria comes from the Italian *malo* (bad) + *aria* (air). The disease was also known as swamp fever, marsh fever, or marsh miasm. Physicians believed the illness was caused by effluvia resulting from vegetable decomposition. It was noted that the disease occurred in warm, wet areas. Woodward states, "It has been observed that the deltas and alluvial margins of great rivers, the borders of tropical streams, the neighborhood of extensive marshes and swamps are the favorite habitations of these maladies, and that they occur in such localities with peculiar violence."[147]

Symptoms of malaria include the typical fever cycles with shaking chills, headache, myalgias (muscle aches), nausea, and vomiting. Severe paroxysms produce pallor, anxiousness, and delirium. Paroxysms of fever and other symptoms last several hours, then subside, only to return again with the next cycle. Some individuals develop a form of chronic malaria with symptoms of general malaise, listlessness, periodic headache, occasional and irregular paroxysms of fever and chills, anorexia, and weight loss.

Malaria is now known to be caused by specific parasitic organisms that invade red blood cells. These parasites are spread from person-to-person via bites from the female *Anopheles* mosquito. These mosquitoes thrive in warm, swampy areas. Three different species of the parasite are responsible for the illness. Quotidian fever is usually caused by *Plasmodium falciparum*, which also, most likely, produced most cases of congestive intermittent fever; tertian fever is caused by *Plasmodium vivax*; quartan fever is caused by *Plasmodium malariae*. Co-infection by more than one species of parasite was also common.

Union doctors cared for 877,324 cases of intermittent fever, with 4287 recorded fatalities. Due to the variety of malarial presentations and non-specific symptoms, the disease was probably greatly under-diagnosed or misdiagnosed, and the actual incidence was probably much higher; most likely nearly doubling the above figures. Chronic malaria was endemic in some areas and often went unreported. Estimates vary, but the incidence of malaria is felt to have been between 224[148] and 522[149] cases per 1000 Union soldiers.

Typho-malarial fever was an illness with features of typhoid fever as well as malaria. As we have seen, typhoid fever characteristically produces a continuous fever whereas malaria produces an intermittent fever. Typho-malarial fevers were described as being predominantly malarial or typhoidal in nature. More than likely, soldiers had one illness or the other, with atypical symptoms, or neither illness, with symptoms due to another cause, or both illnesses at the same time. Union physicians recorded 49,871 cases of typho-malarial fever with 4,059 deaths.

Civil War soldiers succumbed to the same temptations that have lured soldiers in all armies, throughout all of history. Gonorrhea and syphilis were treated fairly commonly, North and South. Union doctors reported 95,833 cases of gonorrhea and 73,382 cases of syphilis. As Dr. Samuel Gross stated, "It is impossible, even under the most rigid discipline, to prevent gonorrhea among soldiers...they will expose themselves, in spite of all that can be done to prevent it, and they often pay a heavy penalty for their indulgence."[150]

Civil War physicians were called upon to treat many other diseases. Many soldiers became exposed to the "childhood diseases" for the first time when they arrived at camp, with resultant outbreaks of measles, mumps, diphtheria, whooping cough, and chickenpox. Union doctors reported 67,763 cases of measles with 4,287 deaths. Mumps was reported 48,128 times with 72 fatalities.[151] The other "childhood" illnesses were about as common.

Epidemic catarrh (common cold), bronchitis, and pneumonia were very common diagnoses made during daily sick call. Rheumatism was a frequently made diagnosis and probably included cases of acute rheumatic fever (secondary to streptococcal throat infections), as well as chronic ailments such as rheumatoid arthritis, osteoarthritis, gout, simple musculoskeletal back pain (lumbago), and other myriad causes of joint and muscle aches.

Scurvy, or the "scorbutic taint", was probably the most commonly treated non-infectious disease. At the time of the Civil War, the exact cause was still unknown. Physicians did recognize that dietary factors were involved. Woodward states, "Of dietic errors, while sameness of food, imperfect cooking, and excess of salt provisions are all aggravating conditions, the absence of fresh vegetable food appears to be the determining cause."[152]
We now know that scurvy is caused by a diet deficient in Vitamin C; a vitamin found chiefly in fruits and vegetables.
Symptoms of scurvy include weakness, fatigue, diarrhea, easy bruisability, and softening of the gums with ulceration and bleeding.

Three diseases known to have decimated armies in the past were fortunately quite rare among soldiers of the Civil War. The incidence of smallpox was reduced by a fairly effective vaccination program. Union statistics show 12,236 cases reported, with 4,717 deaths. Yellow fever, a viral disease spread by the *Aedes aegypti* species of mosquito, was reported by Union doctors only 1,181 times with 409 fatalities. Cholera, caused by the bacterium, *Vibrio cholerae*, was never present in significant numbers.[153]

Somehow, against all odds, a few soldiers did manage to stay healthy. Some of these soldiers attempted to escape military duty by faking illness. Dr. Samuel Gross, in "*A Manual of Military Surgery*," warned physicians to be alert for the possibility of "feigned diseases." Illnesses which were occasionally faked included, "mania and imbecility; deafness; amaurosis; epilepsy; paralysis; hematemesis; hemoptysis; gastritis; dysentery and diarrhea; affections of the heart; rheumatism; lumbago; wry-neck; contractions of the joint; incontinence of urine; bloody urine; opacity of the cornea; edema of the limbs; wounds;

and amputations of the fingers." He suggested testing for feigned paralysis by "tickling the soldier's feet when he is asleep, or threatening him with the hot iron." He cautioned that soldiers might even feign diarrhea or dysentery by "borrowing the discharges of persons actually affected with these diseases."[154]

Medical Therapeutics:

   Hippocrates, the Greek physician and "Father of Medicine", wrote the Hippocratic Oath in about 400 B.C. To this day, the oath continues to be recited as students graduate from medical school. A line from the oath reads as follows: "I will prescribe regimen for the good of my patients according to my ability and my judgment and never do harm to anyone." This concept has been abbreviated into the tenet, "First of all, do no harm."

   There can be no doubt, that some of the therapies used by Civil War physicians caused harm. There can even be no doubt, that some of these therapies actually contributed to, or directly resulted in, the death of their patients. However, there can also be no doubt, that these same physicians were providing the best care they could, within the framework of existing medical knowledge and theory.

   Medical theory had not advanced all that far from the teachings of the Hippocratic School. According to Hippocrates, illness and health were related to the balance between four bodily fluids or "humors"; blood, phlegm, black bile, and yellow bile. If any of the humors were deficient or in excess, they became "unbalanced", resulting in disease. Bleeding, purging, or sweating relieved the excess. Rest, diet, or medicinals made up any deficiency.

   The great Greek physician, Claudius Galen, during the first century A.D., developed and taught a system of medical anatomy, physiology, pathology, symptomatology, and treatment. His system was based on the four humors of Hippocrates. Treatment methods were those utilized by the Hippocratic School. Galen's theories would stand, unchallenged, for over fifteen centuries.

   During the 17th century, the terms acidity, alkalinity, saltiness, tension, and relaxation were used when describing the imbalances that produced illness. Treatment methods remained unchanged from previous.

   During the mid-18th century, a discovery occurred that drastically changed medical theory. Scientists discovered the fact that a muscle contracted when its innervating nerve was pinched. This seemingly minor observation led to revolutionary changes in the concepts of the causes of disease. By the late 1700's, many physicians practicing and lecturing in the great European medical centers proposed their individual theories based on this discovery.

   Dr. William Cullen of Edinburgh, Scotland, believed that nerve irritation could alter the bodily fluids to cause illness. He devised a massive and complex classification of diseases based on his theory.

   Dr. Francis Broussais of Paris, France, founded the doctrine known as broussaisism; "that living matter has but one property, that of contractility, which is excited into action by irritation and becomes quiescent when no irritation is present."[155] He was responsible for the idea that all irritation, and therefore all disease, resulted from inflammation of the gut. All of his treatment methods involved the gastrointestinal tract.

Scottish physician, Dr. John Brown, further refined some of these concepts into a school of thought known as Brownism or brunonianism. According to his hypothesis, all disease resulted from excessive or deficient stimulation. Excessive stimulation resulted in nerve stimulation, muscle spasm, and diseases of excitability. Too little stimulation resulted in lethargy, weakness, or atony. Excitable states were treated by bleeding, purging, sweating, and "low diet". Depressive conditions were treated by stimulants such as alcohol or other drugs, and "high diet."[156]

By 1861, relatively little had changed since the days of Hippocrates. The theories regarding the causes of disease had changed slightly; available treatment methods were basically the same. At the time of the Civil War, diseases were divided into two groups. The dynamic or sthenic diseases were characterized by their excitable state. Symptoms of these diseases included high fever, strong pulse, flushed skin, rapid respirations, agitation, and active delirium. The second group, the adynamic or asthenic diseases, were characterized by their weakened or depressed state. Symptoms included lassitude, weak pulse and respirations, general wasting, and quiet delirium.[157]

Treatment modalities were aimed at either increasing or decreasing the level of "excitability", depending on the presenting symptoms.

Dr. J.J. Woodward, in his introduction to "*Outlines of the Chief Camp Diseases*", pointed out an observation that "a tendency on the part of all the diseases of the troops to assume an adynamic character was observed both by the military surgeons, upon whom their treatment devolved, and by medical men from all parts of the country...."[158] He goes on to state that this trend toward adynamic symptoms had been seen among all the chief camp diseases including malaria, typhoid, measles, bronchitis, pneumonia, diarrhea, and dysentery. As a result "it has been found that depressing therapeutic agents of every character, including blood-letting, antimonials, mecurials, and low diet, have been ill borne, and the majority even of the warmest adherents of such remedies have usually, after some experience, grown exceedingly cautious in their administration or abandoned them altogether."[159]

As the result of trail and error, clinical observation, and a gradual change in medical thought, some of the classic treatments were slowly being abandoned; systemic blood-letting and aggressive purging were no longer considered to be appropriate mainstream medical therapeutics.

Dr. Samuel Gross outlined the general classes of medicinals felt to be of therapeutic benefit:[160]

1. Anodynes: (narcotic pain relievers)-opium and morphine, in various forms.

2. Purgatives (cathartics):-blue mass and calomel (mercury chloride), rhubarb, jalap, compound extract of colocynth, sulfate of magnesia.

3. Depressants (sedatives):-tartrate of antimony and pottassa, ipecacuanaha, and tincture of veratrum viride.

4. <u>Diaphoretics</u>: (produce sweating)-antimony, ipecacuanha, nitrate of potassa, morphia, and Dover's powder (powder of ipecac and opium).
5. <u>Diuretics</u>: (produce urination)-nitrate and carbonate of potassa, and colchicum.
6. <u>Antiperiodics</u>: (antimalarials)-quinine and arsenic.
7. <u>Anesthetics</u>: chloroform and ether.
8. <u>Stimulants</u>: brandy, gin, wine, whisky, rum, and aromatic spirits of ammonia.
9. <u>Astringents</u>: (coagulants used to stop secretions and styptics used to stop bleeding)-acetate of lead, perchloride of iron and alum, tannin, galic acid, and nitrate of silver.
10. <u>Escharotics</u>: (caustics used to cauterize infected tissue)-nitric acid, acid nitrate of mercury, Bennetts's formula, and Vienna paste.
(modern descriptive terms in parentheses)

In "*The Pictorial Encyclopedia of Civil War Medical Instruments and Equipment*", *Volume 1*, Dr. Gordon Dammann lists the standard medicinals contained in the U.S. Army Medical Pannier.[161] Added to this list are the typical uses of these medications.[162]

1. <u>Cantharides</u>: irritant, rubefacient, vesicant. Ground, dried beetle; *Cantharis vesicatoria* (Spanish fly). Used internally as a stimulant. Used externally for therapeutic inflammation and skin blistering (vesicant). Rubefacients produced redness of the skin; believed to divert an irritation from an internal part to the surface.

2. <u>Silver Nitrate</u>: Used internally as a tonic, and as an antispasmodic for epilepsy, chorea, angina pectoris, and other spasmodic diseases. Used internally for gastric discomfort. Used externally as a vesicant and escharotic. Used externally in the treatment of hospital gangrene. Used as a styptic to control minor bleeding and to cauterize mercury-induced oral lesions.

3. <u>Silver Chloride</u>: antiseptic, astringent, styptic.

4. <u>Iodine</u>: corrosive, irritant, desiccant, tonic, diuretic, diaphoretic, disinfectant.

5. <u>Tartar Emetic</u>: Tartrate of antimony and potassium. Alterative (thought to cause a favorable change in the disordered functions of the body), diaphoretic, diuretic, expectorant, purgative, emetic.

6. <u>Mercurous Chloride</u>: Mild chloride of mercury; known commonly as calomel. Purgative, antihelmintic, alterative, emetic. A strong purgative and

powerful irritant. Caused general excitation with increased pulse and increased secretions. Used in gastrointestinal and hepatic disorders. Toxic effects included painful and bleeding gums, tooth loss, and mouth ulcers. Sometimes massive necrosis and tissue loss occurred - "mercurial gangrene" - resulted in disfiguring and disabling injury.

Several U.S. physicians, including U.S. Surgeon General William Hammond, felt the use of this drug should be banned due to its toxic effects.

U.S. Medical Department Circular No.6 was issued in May, 1863, which banned the use of calomel (and tartar emetic). Many politically prominent physicians became outraged at this ban on a drug they'd been using for years. Hammond's opposition to its continued use was one of the factors that led to his political demise.

7. Beef Extract: nutrient. Used in cases of diarrhea and dysentery.

8. Coffee Extract: stimulant. Used in cases of diarrhea and dysentery.

9. Condensed Milk: anti-diarrheal. Used primarily in cases of dysentery.

10. Alcohol: stimulant. Wine, rum, whisky, brandy. Excites the system, renders the pulse full, communicates additional energy to the muscles. Used in almost all cases of shock or debility.

11. Black Tea: astringent, mild stimulant.

12. Spirit of Nitrous Ether: diaphoretic, diuretic, antispasmodic.

13. Alcohol Fortis: "Strong alcohol." Absolute alcohol approaching 100%. Used as a stimulant and rubefacient.

14. Cough Mixture: Syrupy liquid. Various recipes that contained glycerin, vinegar, herbs (flaxseed, horehound, licorice, others), gum arabic, and whiskey.

15. White Sugar: nutrient, antiseptic, demulcent (relieves irritation of mucous membranes).

16. Chloroform: Inhaled anesthetic. Internally used as a sedative, anesthetic.

17. Liniment: Applied to skin as a counterirritant, rubefacient, anodyne, emollient, or cleansing agent. Various recipes that contained belladonna, opium, aconite root, ammonia, capsicum, chloroform, turpentine,

cantharides, camphor. Several different oils used as a base (olive oil, turpentine oil).

18. <u>Syrup of Squill</u>: expectorant, cough relief, emetic, diuretic, purgative.

19. <u>Ammonia water</u>: stimulant, diaphoretic, antacid, rubefacient.

20. <u>Ether</u>: Inhaled anesthetic, antispasmodic. Highly flammable. Chloroform preferred.

21. <u>Opium</u>: Tincture of opium, laudanum. Anodyne.

22. <u>Fluid Extract of Cinchona</u> (Peruvian bark): Tonic. Used for intermittent fever (malaria), syphilis, rheumatism.

23. <u>Fluid Extract of Valerian</u>: stimulant, antispasmodic.

24. <u>Fluid Extract of Ginger</u>: stimulant, carminative (reduces flatulence).

25. <u>Olive Oil</u>: laxative, emollient, liniment base.

26. <u>Oil of Turpentine</u>: Used internally as a stimulant, diuretic, antihelmintic (kills intestinal worms), cathartic. Used externally as a rubefacient, liniment.

27. <u>Glycerin</u>: antiseptic, emollient

28. <u>Paregoric</u>: Camphorated tincture of opium. Relieves cough, diarrhea, nausea, and gastric discomfort.

29. <u>Ferric Sulfate</u>: astringent, styptic. Used as a tonic in solution form.

30. <u>Spirits of Ammonia</u>: Inhaled stimulant. Diluted and used internally as an antispasmodic.

31. <u>Cathartic Pills</u>: Mild laxative. Mixture of colocynth, jalap extract, calomel, and gamhose.

32,33. <u>Ipecac Pills and Ipecac Powder</u>: Also available as a fluid extract. Strong emetic. Used in various forms and concentrations as a stimulant, diaphoretic, or expectorant. Available as a mixture of opium powder and ipecac powder known as "Dover's Powder"; used as an anodyne and diaphoretic.

34. Quinine Sulfate: Used as a treatment for intermittent fever (malaria). Also used to prevent intermittent fever in areas of high incidence. Occasionally used as a general tonic.

35. Potassium Chlorate: Applied topically as a refrigerant (used to cool the skin in fever). Used internally as a diuretic.

36. Potassium Bicarbonate: antacid, diuretic, antilithic (to promote dissolution of kidney stones).

37. Potassium Iodine: expectorant, sialagogue (increases production of saliva).

38. Rochelle Salt: potassium sodium tartrate. Externally used as a refrigerant. Internally used as a purgative.

39. Morphine: anodyne, soporific (induces sleep), diaphoretic. Administered orally, topically on wounds, or occasionally injected subcutaneously with a Wood's syringe.

40. Camphor and Opium Pills: anti-diarrheal, anodyne, antispasmodic.

41. Mercury Pills: also called blue pills or blue mass. Mixture of elemental mercury, powdered licorice, powdered rose leaves, and honey. Used as a laxative, cathartic, and alternative. Milder than calomel.

42. Opium Pills: Also available as a powder or tincture. Best pain reliever available. Used as a sedative, soporific, anodyne, and antispasmodic. Stimulant at low doses. Occasionally used for cough relief. Same routes of administration as morphine.

43. Tannic Acid: Externally used as an astringent. Internally used as an anti-diarrheal.

44. Alum: astringent, styptic, antispasmodic, emetic, purgative. Used as a mouth rinse and gargle for mercury-induced ulcerations.

45. Collodium (Collodion): Flexible, adhesive mixture made by dissolving gun cotton in ether or alcohol. Painted directly over small wounds or abrasions as a protectant. Applied to squares of linen to make adhesive dressings. The thick, gummy base was also mixed with cantharides, iodine, or tannic acid and used as a vesicant, counterirritant, or styptic.

46. Creasote: irritant, anodyne, styptic, antiseptic, escharotic.

47. <u>Fluid Extract of Aconite</u>: sedative

48. <u>Fluid Extract of Colchicum</u> (Colchicine): sedative, anodyne. Used especially for the pain of gouty arthritis.

49. <u>Tincture of Ferric Chloride</u>: potent tonic, diuretic.

50. <u>Lead Acetate</u>: powerful astringent, sedative

51. <u>Zinc Sulfate</u>: Primarily an astringent and styptic. Occasionally used internally as a tonic, emetic, or antispasmodic.

This list is representative of the standard medicinal armamentarium available to the Civil War physician. The pharmacopoeia of the early 1860's included dozens of other medicinals; most commercially prepared, and some prepared by the individual physician. These medicinals included both chemical preparations and herbal remedies; many of which were based on therapies used in traditional folk medicine.

Medications not found in the above list, but apparently used with some frequency, included belladonna (an alkaloid derived from the herb, Nightshade); used as a sedative, diuretic, and diaphoretic. Belladonna's side-effects could be highly toxic and fatal. Commonly used cathartics, not included above, included castor oil and magnesium sulfate (Epsom salts).

Prior to the war, most medicinal manufacturers were located in the North, with stores throughout the United States. The South acquired considerable stockpiles of these medications as the Southern states seceded. Replenishment of supplies for the Confederacy took place via the capture of Union stores, purchases abroad and brought through the coastal blockade, purchases "through the lines" from the North, and medicinals manufactured within the Confederacy.

By order of Confederate Surgeon General Moore, pharmaceutical laboratories were established at various places throughout the South. The largest and most important of these were located in Atlanta and Macon, Georgia; Columbia and Charleston, South Carolina; Charlotte and Lincolnton, North Carolina; Montgomery and Mobile, Alabama; and Tyler, Texas.[163]

Due to the extreme demand for medicinal alcohol, the Confederate government established four government-operated distilleries.

In terms of the actual treatment of disease, each physician had his own preferred methods and medications. Some physicians tended to use medications freely, others hardly at all. Many of the medicines were used to treat symptoms, or perceived underlying "imbalances", rather than well-defined diseases. Therefore, there was considerable physician-to-physician variability in how any given illness or symptom might be treated.

As we have seen, some physicians still adhered to older treatment methods such as bleeding. Systemic blood-letting was rarely used, but many physicians still used local therapies such as leeching, cupping, blistering, or local irritation.

Extreme or violent purging was used less during the war than previously, but the process still had its proponents. Most Civil War physicians still utilized the purging process, but to a milder degree.

Another factor leading to treatment variability was the imprecise diagnostic methods of the era. Physicians made diagnoses based on symptoms and signs; individually or in recognizable syndromes. Some diseases had rather specific symptoms or signs. Others were not very unique, with potential confusion with other diseases. Any given disease might present to them in the early, middle, or late stages, with different findings at each stage. A disease might present with typical findings, making diagnosis easier. Others times, a disease might present in an atypical fashion, making diagnosis more difficult, or leading to the wrong diagnosis entirely.

Civil War physicians made their diagnoses without the benefit of blood tests or X-rays. Even though the thermometer and stethoscope had been invented, they were often not available and only occasionally used. Arriving at the correct diagnosis was a difficult task, and undoubtedly, many errors were made.

In terms of actual treatment modalities available, physicians were somewhat limited. At the core of medical therapeutics were the basic, prevailing concepts of the causes of disease. Therapeutic measures, therefore, were designed to alter those underlying disease-producing conditions. As mentioned above, therapies were usually delivered to reduce or depress a sthenic (excitable or dynamic) state, or to stimulate an asthenic (depressed or adynamic) one. Treatment methods utilized during the war most often fell into the latter category.

The treatment of the sthenic diseases included *antiphlogistic* - "lowering" - therapies and techniques. Sedative medications that were used included aconite, colchicum, lead acetate, opium, and morphine. Antiphlogistic therapies also included localized bleeding, cupping, blistering, and the application of rubefacients; the theory being that superficial bleeding, blistering, or irritation would draw the disease-producing inflammation to the surface, where it would dissipate and allow the underlying illness to resolve.

Aggressive purging, with emetics and strong cathartics, was also a form of antiphlogistic therapy. It was believed that the chemical irritation to the gastrointestinal tract "pulled" inflammation from the internal organs into the gastrointestinal lumen, thereby allowing it to be expelled from the body. Diaphoretics and diuretics were thought to work by similar mechanisms.

As was noted by Woodward and others, utilizing any of the above therapies too aggressively produced undesirable effects. These untoward effects eventually resulted in an adynamic or asthenic state. This fact, along with the observation that most diseases presented with, or eventually developed, adynamic symptoms anyway, led to the diminished use of many of the "depressive" treatment modalities.

As the above lists illustrate, many medications were used as stimulants. Stimulants were used in the treatment of the asthenic or adynamic illnesses. The most commonly used stimulant (and the most commonly used drug, overall) was alcohol. Almost every "depressive" condition, from shock secondary to a gunshot wound, to weakness from dehydration, was treated with doses of alcohol. In fact, alcohol was administered for almost any illness or injury, and any form of beverage alcohol was used. During the war, over 600,000 gallons of medicinal whiskey, alone, were issued by the U.S. government. In May, 1863, the Confederate government estimated an annual need for 200,000 gallons of medicinal alcohol. By 1865, the Confederates were consuming nearly 625,000 gallons per year.[164]

Other stimulants included the various tonics, turpentine oil, valerian and ginger extracts, coffee, and tea.

Treatment of Specific Diseases:

Diarrhea and Dysentery:

As previously discussed, diarrhea and dysentery were the most common diseases of the Civil War. These diseases were also known as Alvine Fluxes, after the Latin *alvus*; meaning belly, and the Latin *fluxus*; to flow. Besides being the most common diseases of the Civil War, they also resulted in the most fatalities.

If there was one group of illnesses for which the well-meaning physicians caused the most harm, this would have to be it.

Standard treatment for the diarrheal illnesses was exactly the opposite of what was required. The usual therapy consisted of early purging. As Woodward states, "A brisk cathartic should be given at the beginning; it serves to remove not only any irritating food, but the secretions of the diseased intestine, which may themselves prove a source of irritation."[165] By the same theory, emetics, diuretics, and diaphoretics were also utilized. These treatment methods only served to further dehydrate an already dehydrated patient. Fortunately, as abdominal cramping became severe, opium or morphine were administered to relieve the pain. These narcotics have the side-effect of producing constipation, which actually provided unexpected therapeutic benefit. Soldiers were also administered any of several tonics to improve their strength.

Systemic blood-letting had been a standard treatment for the fluxes since the days of Hippocrates and Galen. With a change in the theory of the cause of the disease, from "bad humors" to internal excitation or inflammation, systemic blood-letting was rarely used, for the treatment of diarrhea, by the time of the Civil War. Writing in "*The Medical and Surgical History of the War of the Rebellion*", J.J. Woodward presents his view on the subject of blood-letting in the treatment of diarrhea:

> "Is this practice necessary or justifiable? I cannot think so. If a sufficient quantity of blood be drawn in this way to produce any constitutional impression, it can only diminish the natural powers of resistance and thus indirectly add to the dangers of the disease...No more in this than in other inflammations is any considerable loss of blood aught but injurious...local, as well as general blood-letting should be abandoned, for it is a delusion to imagine that we can, by their means, either check or modify for the better the course of the disease."[166]

However, in the treatment of diarrhea or dysentery, some physicians continued to use local blood-letting measures such as wet or dry cups, or leeches, applied to the abdomen.

Other unusual therapies, used in the treatment of the diarrheal illnesses, included astringent enemas, leeches to the anus, and attempts to chemically cauterize the rectum and anus.

Given time, most infectious diarrhea/dysentery is self-limited, and the soldier would eventually recover. As the war progressed, and sanitation measures and personal hygiene improved, the incidence of the diarrhea/dysentery illnesses decreased. General measures that led to this improvement included reduced crowding, better sources of drinking water (less fecal contamination), designated camp cooks (better personal hygiene than the average soldier), and better placement, construction, and utilization of latrines.

Typhoid Fever:

Typhoid fever produced the second most common cause of death by disease. The treatment of typhoid fever, and the other Continued Fevers, included emetics and cathartics to rid the body of irritating substances. These fevers were felt to be asthenic or adynamic illnesses, and therefore, were treated with stimulants of various types. Cold applications, sponge baths with water, or water and alcohol, and topical refrigerants were used to reduce fever. Mercurials, oil of turpentine, abdominal cupping or leeches, blistering agents, and rubefacients were among other remedies utilized.

General measures used in the treatment of the Continued Fevers included isolation, bedrest, avoidance of hot or cold environmental temperatures, and liquid or bland diets.

Intermittent Fever (Malaria):

Cinchona is the dried bark of various species of the Cinchona tree, native to South America. Its chemical composition includes a number of alkaloids, the most prevalent of which is quinine.

The first written record of the use of Cinchona bark, in the treatment of febrile illness, dates back to 1633. Most likely, the bark had been used medicinally for hundreds of years prior to that date. In 1820, quinine was extracted from the bark in purified form. Quinine's efficacy in the treatment of intermittent fever was well-established by 1861. Quinine is now known to be a specific anti-malarial agent. Its use during the Civil War, as a treatment for the malarial fevers, represents one of the few instances where the treatment rendered actually produced true therapeutic benefit.

Unfortunately, other therapies used in the treatment of malaria were not so efficacious. These included purging, blood-letting, calomel, and turpentine.

Document No. 31, issued by the U.S. Sanitary Commission in late 1861, recommended the use of quinine as a preventative measure in areas where the disease was prevalent.[167]

Confederate Medical Inspector Joseph Jones, aware of the prophylactic use of quinine by English seamen stationed off the African coast, recommended such use of the drug for Southern troops.[168]

Due to its short supply, and the large quantities of the drug required for the treatment of acute malaria, quinine was never used extensively, by either side, for malarial prophylaxis. However, it is an effective agent for this purpose, and continues to be used to this day.

Venereal Diseases:

Gonorrhea is caused by the bacterium, *Neisseria gonorrhea*. Acutely, it produces an irritating, copious, thick penile discharge. Chronically, gonorrhea may become disseminated and produce a form of arthritis. It can also result in urethral strictures.

During the Civil War, treatment methods included penile "injections" (irrigation) with various compounds, such as solutions of chlorate of potash, chloride of zinc, silver nitrate, mercury, or lead.[169] Additional therapies included rest, cathartics, refrigerants, and low (bland) diet. Remedies used in the South also included poke roots or berries, elder, wild sarsaparilla, sassafras, jessamine, and prickly ash. One Southern surgeon discovered that "silk weed root put in whiskey and drank, giving at the same time pills of rosin from the pine tree, with very small pieces of blue vitrol" would cure stubborn cases of gonorrhea.[170]

Syphilis is caused by the microbe, *Treponema pallidum*. Syphilitic infection progresses through three stages. Primary (acute) syphilis is characterized by small painless ulcers (chancres), usually found on the penis. These chancres spontaneously heal over the course of several weeks. Four to ten weeks later the symptoms of secondary syphilis develop. Secondary symptoms include fever, malaise, lymphadenopathy (swollen lymph nodes), and rash. These symptoms gradually subside and the disease then enters a long latent phase. Most individuals never go on to develop tertiary syphilis, however, the one-third that do suffer severe consequences. Tertiary syphilis may develop many years after the first two stages. In the tertiary stage, the infection involves the skin and internal organs (gummas), cardiovascular system, and nervous system, with devastating effects. Large skin tumors develop, inflammation of the aorta occurs with heart valve problems and the formation of aortic aneurysms, and the patient may develop profound dementia and other crippling neurologic symptoms.

Treatment of syphilis, by Civil War physicians, included cauterization of the primary chancre, emetics and cathartics, mercurials, and a variety of other medicinals.

Unfortunately, none of the above therapies for gonorrhea or syphilis actually cured either disease. Soldiers continued to harbor the infectious gonorrhea and syphilis-causing organisms. The diseases were subsequently spread to any future sexual partners, including their wives and girlfriends back home. These sexual partners then became chronically infected.

If the infected women became pregnant, their babies contracted the infections as well. Gonorrheal infection occurs as the infant passes through the birth canal. It primarily causes an infection of the lining around the eyes called gonorrheal ophthalmia. This infection can cause corneal ulcers leading to corneal scarring and blindness.

Syphilis infects the fetus in the uterus, via the placenta. Infected mothers transmit syphilis to their babies 60-80% of the time. Congenital syphilis causes skin lesions, enlargement of the liver and spleen, meningitis, seizures, and mental retardation, as well as other congenital abnormalities.

There are no statistics on the number of women, and subsequent children, infected with venereal disease. Considering the fact that Union physicians treated 170,000 reported cases of venereal disease - this number does not include any Confederate soldiers or soldiers that did not seek treatment - the figures must be staggering.

One Civil War researcher estimated that one-third of the men who died in Union and Confederate veteran's homes were killed by the late stages of venereal disease.[171]

Parasitic Infections:

Civil War soldiers were plagued by a variety of parasitic infestations. Skin infestations were extremely common and exceedingly bothersome. Both scabies (caused by the itch mite, *Scarcoptes scabiei*) and pediculosis (caused by the body louse, *Pediculus* or *Phthirus corporis*) were nearly ubiquitous. As George Adams states, in "*Doctors in Blue*", "In the Civil War, scratching was as common as body lice, fleas, and mosquitoes."[172] A multi-factorial, chronic, itchy condition, suffered by almost all soldiers, was referred to as "camp itch." Camp itch resulted from the above mentioned parasitic infestations along with poor personal hygiene.

Treatment for camp itch included sulfur, arsenic, or alkaline baths. Bathing with a solution made by boiling poke root, broom straw, or slippery elm, in water, was also tried. One Confederate assistant surgeon made a therapeutic ointment "from the inner bark of the elder, lard, sweet gum, basilican ointment, olive oil, and sulfur flour."[173] Most Civil War soldiers just learned to live with the problem.

Civil War soldiers were also infested with a variety of intestinal worms. These included round worms, hookworms, pinworms, whipworms, and tapeworms.

Treatments (antihelmintics) included oil of turpentine, calomel, arsenic, enemas and cathartics.

Medical Therapeutics in Summary:

The vast majority of medications prescribed by Civil War physicians were of absolutely no therapeutic benefit. In many cases, ill soldiers were only made worse by the medicines administered to them.

Several of the medications used were quite toxic and resulted in serious side-effects. Toxic medications included calomel and other preparations of mercury, arsenic, belladonna, tartar emetic and other antimonials, lead acetate, and cantharides.

Other medications caused harm while producing their supposed therapeutic benefit. These included the emetics, purgatives/cathartics, diaphoretics, and diuretics. The adverse effect of these drugs was caused by the further depletion of fluids and electrolytes, in soldiers already seriously dehydrated by fever, vomiting, and diarrhea.

Vesicants, blistering agents, rubefacients, leeches, cups, and other similar local therapies produced no therapeutic benefits, and may have caused harm if they resulted in secondary infection.

Alcohol was the most commonly prescribed medicine used during the Civil War. It was of absolutely no benefit in the way it was prescribed. Alcohol was felt to be a stimulant, and was given in small doses to combat shock, or to "stimulate" any depressive condition. In larger oral doses, it could have been used as a pain reliever, sedative, or amnesiac. Topically, it could have been used as an antiseptic. Unfortunately, it was rarely used for any of those purposes.

Of all the medications commonly prescribed by Civil War physicians, only six actually produced therapeutic benefit toward the illness or condition for which they were used. These included the narcotics - morphine and opium; the general anesthetics - chloroform and ether; the antiseptic - bromine; and the anti-malarial agent - quinine.

The narcotics - morphine and opium - were powerful analgesics, and undoubtedly eased the suffering of countless soldiers. The most effective route of administration was by injection, but unfortunately, the necessary equipment (Wood's syringe) was not often available. The next best route was by placement of the narcotic into a fresh wound, where it could be absorbed directly into the blood stream. The least effective route - administration by mouth - was the most commonly used. Union records account for the use of 2,841,596 ounces of tincture of opium or opium powder, and almost a half a million opium pills.[174]

Both chloroform and ether are quite effective general anesthetics. They are relatively safe when administered by the open-drop technique used in the Civil War. Utilizing this technique, a cone of cloth was soaked with the anesthetic agent. The cloth was then positioned over the patient's nose and mouth. When the patient fell asleep, the cloth was removed, and the patient was then allowed to breath fresh air. If the patient began to wake prematurely, the cloth was reapplied.

At the start of the war, some very prominent surgeons, including Dr. Samuel Gross, author of "*A Manual of Military Surgery*", felt that anesthetics were often unnecessary. In his own words, "...so long as the vital powers are depressed and the mind is bewildered by shock, or loss of blood, their administration will hardly be safe...moreover, it is astonishing what little suffering the patient generally experiences, when in this condition, even from a severe wound or operation."[175] In spite of a few similar misgivings, general anesthesia was extensively utilized by both Union and Confederate surgeons. A soldier undergoing a significant operation or procedure, without benefit of anesthesia, was a rare event. Union records document the use of general anesthesia in over 80,000 cases. Chloroform was used 76% of the time; ether 14%; and a mix of the two, 9%. Anesthesia-related deaths occurred thirty-seven times from chloroform, four from ether, and twice from the combined agent.[176] Confederate Surgeon Hunter Holmes McGuire, medical director of Stonewall Jackson's corps, stated that, although chloroform was administered over 28,000 times in his corps, "no death was ever ascribed to its use."[177]

Fortunately for the Civil War soldier, the use of general anesthetics quickly became "standard of care."

Bromine was widely used in the treatment of hospital gangrene; more so in the latter stages of the war. Initially sprayed into the air to combat "effluvia", it gradually was used more and more as a topical antiseptic. Vocal advocates of its use included the U.S. Medical Department, the U.S. Sanitary Commission, and several prominent U.S. surgeons.

Quinine had been used in the treatment of malaria for hundreds of years prior to 1861. It continued to be used extensively for this purpose during the Civil War. Union records document the use of 2,072,040 ounces of cinchona (quinine) products.[178]

Of considerable significance was the adoption of quinine, as a prophylactic medication, to prevent malaria in endemic areas. This practice was endorsed by both Union and Confederate physicians. Document 31 of the U.S. Sanitary Commission endorsed and instructed physicians on its use in this respect.[179]

In light of the dozens of medications prescribed by Civil War physicians, it seems almost incomprehensible that only about half a dozen actually did what they were prescribed to do. Most did nothing, and many caused irreversible harm or even death. One must keep in mind, however, the erroneous medical theories of the 1860's - the underlying concepts that drove medical therapeutics. Medical treatment was based on these principles, in conjunction with the therapies utilized in standard folk medicine, along with traditional remedies left over from the days of Hippocrates and Galen. The controlled, scientific studies of today, along with evidence and outcome-based medicine, lay far in the unforseeable future.

Dr. Oliver Wendell Holmes astonished an 1860 audience of New England physicians by declaring, "...if the whole materia medica, as now used, could sink to the bottom of the sea, it would be all the better for mankind - and all the worse for the fishes."[180]

Perhaps, he was not so far off.

CONCLUSION:

At the beginning of the Civil War, the United States Government included a Medical Department that was ineffective and obsolete. The initial appointees to the postion of U.S. Surgeon General were unable to comprehend the magnitude of the task before them, and they were unwilling to adapt and change, in order to meet the medical needs of a massive army at war. In 1861, the U.S. Medical Department included just over one hundred doctors; one-fourth of these would quit to side with the South. By the end of the war, nearly twenty thousand doctors, in the North and South combined, saw military duty. New programs were developed in the areas of ambulance transport, field hospital care, medical supply, and the building of general hospitals. Civilian groups were organized to help provide supplies and improve medical care. Nursing, as a profession, was instituted to provide care in the general hospitals. This phenomenal change in the military medical system stemmed from changes that occurred at all levels, including the central government, the general public, and the individual practicing physicians, on both sides of the conflict.

The appointment of Dr. William A. Hammond, in April 1862, as U.S. Surgeon General, proved to be the turning point for the U.S. Medical Department. Under Hammond, the Union's medical system began to perform effectively. He appointed qualified and efficient medical directors, and provided for adequate numbers of trained staff to provide medical and surgical care. He then demanded that they be paid and promoted appropriately. He pushed for the construction of new and improved pavilion hospitals and saw that they received adequate supplies. Hammond proposed that the Medical Department take over from the Quartermaster Corps, the control of ambulances and medical supply trains, the construction of hospitals, and the supply of foodstuffs for the hospitals. He was outspoken against harmful medications such as calomel and tartar emetic - much to the chagrin of the established (and out-dated) medical community. Hammond's other achievements included the encouragement of the collection of surgical and pathological specimens for the establishment of the Army Medical Museum, and the careful filing of medical case-reports for later publication as *"The Medical and Surgical History of the War of the Rebellion."* Hammond's successor, Joseph K. Barnes, would see these two projects to completion (and is often given credit for them), but the original impetus came from Hammond himself.
   Hammond's greatest fault appears to have been a certain lack of tack, in a very political world run by "old school" physicians and politicians. After being dismissed on flimsy and trumped-up charges, Hammond was vindicated in 1879, when the charges against him were annulled. After the war, Hammond became an expert on mental and nervous diseases, and was quite successful, both professionally and financially.
   One of Hammond's greatest successes was the appointment of Dr. Jonathan A. Letterman as Medical Director of the Army of the Potomac. Under Letterman, the U.S. Medical Department developed a truly functional and efficient ambulance corps, medical supply plan, and field hospital system. After the war, Letterman took a position in the California office of the Pennsylvania Railroad, but stayed with that firm only a short period of time. He resumed his medical practice, and published his memoirs, *"Medical*

Recollections of the Army of the Potomac", in 1866. In 1867, he was elected Coroner of the City and County of San Francisco, and also served as Coroner of the State of California. He died in San Francisco, in 1872, at the age of forty-seven.[181]

The Medical Department of the Confederate States of America did not even exist until February 26, 1861. Perhaps the fact that this new department did not have to function within the constraints of old rules, regulations, and traditions was an advantage that the North did not share. The Confederate Medical Department had a specific task at hand, and would design a system to fulfill that need.

The Confederate Government found a very able Surgeon General in Dr. Samuel Preston Moore. He had been an assistant surgeon in the regular army, and had served in the Mexican War. He left the U.S. Medical Department to join the Southern cause, along with about twenty-five other U.S. Army physicians. From this core group, Moore would build the Confederate Medical Department. He proved himself a capable administrator and organizer, and he designed, developed, and staffed, a very efficient and effective medical system. Moore instituted an examination process to weed out incompetent physicians, and he encouraged the dissemination of medical information via professional meetings and through medical publications. He provided for the establishment of several pharmaceutical laboratories throughout the South, in the hopes that plants, indigenous to the South, could provide the Confederacy's medicinal needs. He is often given credit for the development of the pavilion hospital, used by both sides during the war, and still in use today.

After the war, Moore left medical practice and served on the Richmond, Virginia school board for twenty-five years.

Samuel H. Stout, Medical Director of the Army of the Tennessee, and Lafayette Guild, Medical Director of the Army of Northern Virginia, were Surgeon General Moore's most capable and inventive medical directors.

Under Stout, a number of excellent general hospitals were constructed in the West. His hospitals were characterized by their mobility; a very necessary trait as they followed an army always on the move. Stout's general hospitals were considered, by many contemporaries, to be the finest in the Confederacy.

Like Moore, after the war, Stout became involved in education. He is given credit for establishing the public school system in Atlanta, Georgia. He helped found the medical department at the University of Dallas, and became Dean of the faculty. He died in 1903, at the age of eighty-two.

Lafayette Guild was perhaps the South's most far-sighted medical director. Guild developed systems of ambulance transport, medical supply, and field hospitals - performing in a similar fashion to the Union's Jonathan Letterman. Guild seems to have had a say in almost all medical and surgical aspects of the Confederate Army. Unfortunately, shortages of supplies and personnel caused the final results to often fall short of his hopes and expectations.

After the war, Lafayette Guild became quarantine inspector for the port of Mobile, Alabama. He died in 1870, at the age of forty-five.

A truly remarkable occurrence, throughout the war, was the transformation of thousands of rural general practitioners into military surgeons. In their private practices, surgical procedures had usually been minor and relatively infrequent. Within a short period of time, these same doctors were treating devastating war wounds in alarming numbers. Education for these physicians was on-the-job. Numerous texts were written by prominent physicians on matters relating to military medicine and surgery. Professional journals were written on subjects of importance to military physicians. These publications were studied intently by the new surgeons, but most of their training would occur while actually caring for the wounded. Huge numbers of casualties, many presenting with massive trauma, provided the necessary experience. As the war went on, and medical care was provided at the division or corps level, surgeons showing exceptional skill tended to perform most of the surgeries. Other physicians tended to care for soldiers with illnesses. The division of modern medical practice into the specialties of surgery and internal medicine, can be traced back to these Civil War roots.

As a result of the tremendous number of extremity injuries which required orthopedic surgery, some orthopedic surgical techniques and treatment methods developed during the Civil War are still in use today. Certain aspects of splinting techniques and traction methods (i.e., Buck's traction) have changed very little. Just seven years after the war, orthopedic surgery began to be recognized as a distinct specialty; a direct result of the overwhelming number of cases of extremity trauma that occurred during the Civil War.

The specialty of maxillo-facial surgery had its beginnings in a military hospital in Atlanta, where Dr. James Baxter Bean developed the first inter-dental splint to be used in fractures of the face.

The medical experience of the Civil War brought about changes in day-to-day medical and surgical practice. Traditional therapies such as systemic blood-letting and aggressive purging were abandoned. Local bleeding using leeches, scarificators, and cups was falling out of favor. Toxic medications such as calomel and tartar emetic were condemned. Extensive surgical experience resulted in refined surgical techniques. The era of antisepsis was ushered in by the use of bromine in the treatment of hospital gangrene. Civil War physicians had thousands upon thousands of case-studies on which to gauge the effectiveness of certain surgical procedures or medical therapies. By individual experience, published reports, and dissemination by word-of-mouth, these observations led to changes in standard medical and surgical practices. Antiquated, traditional remedies began to be superseded by treatment methods proven by trial-and-error and observation.

In the United States, the profession of nursing began with the women recruited by Dorthea Dix to tend for ill and injured Civil War soldiers. The Confederacy went so far as to recommend that women be employed as nurses whenever possible. By 1865, nurses had firmly established their place in the overall provision of medical care.

After the war, formal schools of nursing were founded in many general hospitals. Dorthea Dix resumed her pre-war role in the founding of mental institutions and improving care for the mentally ill. Dix died in Trenton, New Jersey, in 1887, at the age of eighty-four.

Prior to the Civil War, ill or injured patients were generally cared for in their homes, with nursing duties being provided by family members. Actual medical evaluation and treatment was provided during house calls made by the family doctor. Hospitals were institutions that provided care for the homeless and destitute. Traditionally, Catholic sisters provided the nursing care at these facilities.

During the war, approximately 350 general hospitals were constructed in many cities throughout the North and South. After the war, the U.S. Government gradually pulled its medical staff from these institutions. As soldiers recovered and were discharged, the local populations began to use the hospitals for their own care. Many of these hospitals were administered by the Catholic sisters that had staffed the facility during the war. With the development of formal nursing training, many also began to employ professional lay nurses. This change marked the beginning of in-patient, hospital-based, medical care for the general public.

In 1881, the Civil War battlefield relief work of Clara Barton would lead to the formation of the American National Red Cross. Barton served as the President of the American Red Cross until 1904. Barton played an instrumental role in the adoption of neutrality agreements for medical personnel at the first Geneva Convention, in 1864. In 1882, Barton succeeded in having the United States sign the Geneva Agreement on the treatment of the sick, wounded, and dead in battle, and the handling of prisoners of war. Barton also conducted relief work during the Spanish-American War (1898). She was the author of several books on the subject of the Red Cross. Prior to the Civil War, she had worked as a schoolteacher and as a clerk in the U.S. Patent Office in Washington, D.C. The Civil War marked the turning-point in Clara Barton's career. Barton died in Glen Echo, Maryland, in 1912, at the age of ninety.

The extraordinary relief work of the U.S. Sanitary Commission, the United States Christian Commission, and the various aid and relief societies of the South, did much to ease the suffering of ill and injured soldiers.

Insistence, by the U.S. Sanitary Commission, on proper camp hygiene and sanitation led to a significant improvement in the health of the individual soldier.

Without the role these relief agencies played in bringing public support (and money) to the military medical effort, neither the Union nor Confederate Medical Departments would have been able to provide an acceptable level of medical care.

Members of the Medical Departments of the Union and Confederate governments realized the importance of accurate documentation of medical and surgical cases, keeping good written records, and filing case-reports in a central location. Both sides planned to accumulate these records into publications at the end of the war. Union Surgeon General William Hammond initiated the project for the North; his successor, Joseph Barnes, saw it through to completion.

Confederate Surgeon General Samuel Moore had similar plans, and Medical Director Samuel Stout was a vocal advocate of the necessity of documenting and filing case-reports. Unfortunately, most of the records of the Confederate Medical Department were lost in the burning of Richmond at the end of the war. The surviving records from the Confederacy are mainly those that were still in the hands of individual physicians in 1865.

It should be noted that Civil War medical records must be viewed with some caution. Without doubt, the surviving case-reports do provide valuable insight into the medical and surgical treatment methods of the war. However, the statistics need to be viewed with some skepticism. These statistics relied on case-reports and other documents, which had to be filled-out and sent to the medical department. These forms were usually completed by physicians working in the general hospitals. There were also forms to be filled-out by the regimental surgeons after daily sick-call. Filling out paperwork was no more pleasant a task at the time of the Civil War than it is now, and everything had to literally be filled-out and tabulated by hand. Needless to say, some information was never recorded, and some was never sent to Washington to be available for tabulation, at the end of the war.

One also needs to be aware that not all ill soldiers presented to the physician for treatment. War wounds generally required the attention of the surgeon, but many soldiers did not trust doctors to provide care for medical illness (perhaps rightly so, in many instances). These soldiers often tried various home remedies they concocted themselves, or which were made up by their comrades. It is also a fact that many soldiers, North and South, deserted the army and went home for treatment when they were ill. These cases never made it into the statistical records.

Another factor leading to potential error in the statistics, is the imprecise diagnostic methods of the day. Diagnoses were based solely on symptoms and physical findings, without the benefit of X-rays or laboratory tests. Diseases did not always present with characteristic signs and symptoms, and many different diseases could present with similar findings. These factors led to variations (or error) in diagnosis among various physicians.

However, as an overall view of medical and surgical care, and a general analysis of the frequency of certain conditions and diseases, these records are invaluable. The amount of information that was accumulated and tabulated, long before the electronic age, is truly remarkable.

On June 9, 1862, the U.S. Surgeon General's office issued a circular announcing its intention to prepare a medical and surgical history of the war. Medical directors were instructed to forward duplicates of their records to the Surgeon General's office in Washington, D.C. Dr. John H. Brinton - who had been Grant's medical director in the West and was a cousin of General George B. ("Brinton") McClellan's - was originally assigned the task of accumulating the surgical records. Later, Dr. George A. Otis would be given this assignment. The job of accumulating the medical records was given to Dr. J.J. Woodward.

The Surgeon General's office also planned the development of the Army Medical Museum, which would require the collection of pathologic specimens. A circular was distributed asking surgeons to send their specimens to Washington. The Surgeon General specifically requested "excised bones with fractures - simple and compound; diseased bones and joints; stumps; examples of exit and entrance wounds - round ball and conical ball; wounds of vessels and nerves; wounded viscera; and photographs of extraordinary injuries."[182] These specimens were tagged with case-reports and clinical narratives, and then sent to Washington; usually preserved in barrels of whiskey or other alcohol. Stories circulated that soldiers unwittingly tapped into these barrels, along the route to Washington, to drink a bit of the whiskey - never knowing what additional items the barrels contained. An unsubstantiated rumor - but interesting, never-the-less.

On June 8, 1868, Congress approved the appropriation of funds to publish *"The Medical and Surgical History of the War of the Rebellion* (1861-1865)."* This phenomenal work was published in six massive volumes between 1870 and 1888. It contains thousands of case-reports, tabulated statistics on illnesses, injuries, and causes of death, illustrations, diagrams, photographs of soldiers with war wounds, and photographs of pathologic specimens. This work is widely regarded as the first important American academic medical publication, and it received high acclaim by the international medical community.

The *"Medical and Surgical History of the War of the Rebellion"* was reviewed by Rudolph Virchow - the world-renown German pathologist and statesman - in 1870. He stated:

> "Whoever takes up and reads the extensive publications of the American medical staff will be constantly astonished at the wealth of experience found therein. The greatest exactness of detail, careful statistics, even in the smallest matters, and a scholarly statement embracing all sides of medical experience are here united, in order to preserve and transmit to contemporaries and posterity in the greatest possible completeness, the knowledge purchased at so vast an expense."[183]

The photographic record of the surgical aspects of the Civil War was prepared by Dr. George A. Otis and was published between 1865 and 1872, in eight massive volumes entitled, *"Photographs of Surgical Cases and Specimens; Taken at the Army Medical Museum."*

This work includes hundreds of photographs of injured soldiers, each displaying their war wounds, and photographs of related pathologic specimens. A clinical narrative accompanies each photograph.

In addition to these governmental works, several Civil War surgeons wrote memoirs of their own personal experiences. Also, several medical and surgical textbooks were written in the post-war years, teaching the lessons learned during the conflict. These included, "*A Practical Treatise on Fractures and Dislocations*" and "*A Treatise on Military Surgery and Hygiene*" both by Dr. Frank H. Hamilton, and "*Gunshot Wounds and Other Injuries of Nerves*" by S.W. Mitchell, Morehouse, and Keen. Medical journals discussed numerous aspects of Civil War medicine, long after the war.

The Civil War ended in 1865 taking 600,000 young Americans with it. The war also produced approximately 500,000 men with permanent disabilities. It is estimated that nearly 50,000 men had a limb amputated during the war. Those that survived their surgery returned home, missing an amputated arm, leg, hand, or foot. After the war, the individual states and the U.S. Government appropriated funds to help soldiers purchase prosthetic limbs. In January, 1864, the Confederacy established the Association for the Relief of Maimed Soldiers. It's purpose - "to supply artificial limbs for all officers, soldiers, and seamen who have been maimed in the service of their country..."[184] By October, 1864, the organization had spent $125,000 to purchase 499 artificial limbs. Eventually, the organization would supply at least 769 soldiers with artificial limbs. State organizations often provided transportation to and from the prosthesis supplier, as well as financial assistance in purchasing the prosthesis itself. The U.S. Government provided soldiers with vouchers to use toward the purchase of an artificial limb. The dollar amount of the voucher depended on the prosthetic limb needed - a voucher for an artificial leg was worth about $75.00. Due to the huge number of prostheses required and manufactured, rapid advances were made in the details and mechanics of their construction. Although some were as crude and cheap as a simple wooden "peg-leg", others were fashioned of wood and metal, with hinged joints, flexible feet, and functional fingers. The art and science of prosthetic device design advanced significantly as a result of the Civil War.

The Civil War took place at the dawn of modern medicine. Within a few short years after the war, medical advances and discoveries occurred which would have reduced the mortality rate of the war, significantly. Joseph Lister published his landmark work on surgical antisepsis in 1867. He performed the first open-reduction and internal-fixation of a fracture, using aseptic surgical technique, in 1877. In 1878, Robert Koch, a German bacteriologist, discovered the role that bacteria play in causing disease. By 1883, he had identified the bacteria that cause tuberculosis and cholera. In short order, the infectious etiologies of many diseases were identified. Medical theories of bad humors, tainted blood, miasmas, and effluvia were gone forever. In 1895, a German physicist working at the University of Wurzburg, Wilhelm Conrad Roentgen, discovered X-rays. The fundamentals of modern medicine were completed with the addition of antibiotic therapy - sulfa during WW I and penicillin during WW II.

In spite of the lack of medical knowledge under which the Civil War physician worked, the mortality rate of the Civil War had significantly improved from previous wars. The death rate from disease, during the Civil War, was 65 deaths per 1,000 troops. During the Mexican War (1846-1848), the death rate among American troops was 110 deaths per 1,000 troops. During the Crimean War (1854-1856), the death rate due to disease, among the British, French, and Russian soldiers, averaged 278 deaths per 1,000 troops. The gunshot wound mortality of 14% during the Civil War, compares with a 20% mortality during the Crimean War.[185]

Civil War doctors were subjected to the same hazards that confronted the common soldier. Of the 12,344 doctors who served as physicians in the Union Army, statistics reveal that 32 were killed in battle, 9 were killed in accidents, 83 were wounded in action, 10 died from those wounds, and 285 died from disease.

Comparable statistics for the Confederate Medical Department are not available, but most likely are proportionately similar.

Now the sun's gone to hell
And the moon's riding high
Let me bid you farewell
Every man has to die
But it's written in the starlight
And every line on your palm
We're fools to make war
On our brothers in arms

From the song, *Brothers in Arms*
Performed by Dire Straits
Lyrics by Mark Knopfler

- FOOTNOTES -

[1]Coggins, J., *Arms and Equipment of the Civil War*, Wilmington, NC, Broadfoot
Publishing Co., 1962, reprinted 1990. p 38.

[2]Ibid. p 38.

[3]McHenry, R., General Editor, *The New Encyclopedia Britannica*, Chicago, IL,
Encyclopedia Britannica, Inc., 1992. Vol. 10. p 627.

[4]Ibid. Vol. 9. p 190.

[5]Ibid. Vol. 7. p 394.

[6]Adams, G.W., *Doctors in Blue*, New York, NY, Collier Books., 1961. p 6, 13, 14.

[7]Ibid. p 30.

[8]Duncan, L.C., "The Days Gone By: The Strange Case of Surgeon General Hammond,"
The Military Surgeon, January, 1929. p 99.

[9]Adams, *Doctors in Blue*. p 33.

[10]Duncan, The Strange Case of Surgeon General Hammond, *The Military Surgeon*,
p 103.

[11]Ibid. p 99.

[12]Ibid. p 110.

[13]Ibid. p 100.

[14]Adams, *Doctors in Blue*. p 36.

[15]Duncan, The Strange Case of Surgeon General Hammond, *The Military Surgeon*,
p 101.

[16]Ibid. p 107.

[17]Ibid. p 109.

[18]Ibid. p 257.

[19]Ibid. p 101.

[20]Adams, *Doctors in Blue*. p 43.

[21]Duncan, The Strange Case of Surgeon General Hammond, *The Military Surgeon*.
p 261.

[22]Cunningham, H.H., *Doctors in Gray*, Baton Rouge, LA, Louisiana State University
Press, 1993. p 27, 28, 29.

[23]Adams, *Doctors in Blue*. p 12.

[24]Ibid. p 17.

[25]Ibid. p 152.

[26]Ibid. p 47.

[27]Cunningham, *Doctors in Gray*. p 27.

[28]Ibid. p 21, 22.

[29]Ibid. p 29.

[30]Denney, R.E., *Civil War Medicine*, New York, NY, Sterling Publishing Co., Inc., 1994.
p 11.

[31]Bollet, A.J., M.D., Lessons from Medical History-Civil War Medicine: In the Beginning,
Resident and Staff Physician, October 1997. p 20.

[32]Adams, *Doctors in Blue*. p 15.

[33]Bollet, Lessons from Medical History-Civil War Medicine: In the Beginning,
Resident and Staff Physician. p 20.

[34] Adams, *Doctors in Blue.* p 13.

[35] Miller, F.T., *The Photographic History of the Civil War*, Volume 7, New York, NY, Thomas Yoseloff, Inc., 1957. p 329.

[36] Adams, *Doctors in Blue.* p 29.

[37] *The Civil War CD-ROM*, The War of the Rebellion: A Compilation of the Official Records of the Union and Confederate Armies, Carmel, IN, Guild Press of Indiana, Inc.,1997.

[38] Miller, *The Photographic History of the Civil War*, Volume 7. p 338.

[39] *The Documents of the United States Sanitary Commission*, 2 Volumes, New York, NY, 1866.

[40] Ibid.

[41] *The Civil War CD-ROM.*

[42] Miller, *The Photographic History of the Civil War*, Volume 7. p 344.

[43] Woodward, J.J., M.D., *The Hospital Steward's Manual*, San Francisco, CA, Norman Publishing, 1991. Reprint of 1862 original. p 20.

[44] Ibid. p 319.

[45] Cunningham, *Doctors in Gray.* p 75.

[46] Adams, *Doctors in Blue.* p 153.

[47] Ibid. p 154.

[48] Woodward, *The Hospital Steward's Manual.* p 54.

[49] Adams, *Doctors in Blue.* p 160.

[50] Fitzpatrick, M.F., The Mercy Brigade, *Civil War Times Illustrated*, October, 1997. p 36.

[51] Miller, *The Photographic History of the Civil War*, Volume 7. p 228.

[52] Cunningham, *Doctors in Gray.* p 131.

[53] Barber, L.W., *Army Memoirs of Lucius W. Barber*, Time-Life Books, Inc., 1984. Reprint of 1894 original. p 56.

[54] *The Civil War CD-ROM.*

[55] Cunningham, *Doctors in Gray.* p 115.

[56] Miller, *The Photographic History of the Civil War*, Volume 7. p 302.

[57] Duncan, L.C., Evolution of the Ambulance Corps and Field Hospital, *The Military Surgeon*, March, 1913. p 224.

[58] Adams, *Doctors in Blue.* p 27.

[59] Duncan, Evolution of the Ambulance Corps and Field Hospital, *The Military Surgeon*, p 226.

[60] Ibid. p 226.

[61] Ibid. p 234.

[62] Adams, *Doctors in Blue.* p 70.

[63] Ibid. p 72.

[64] Ibid. p 73.

[65] Ibid. p 79.

[66] Duncan, Evolution of the Ambulance Corps and Field Hospital, *The Military Surgeon*, p 248.

[67] Adams, *Doctors in Blue.* p 81.

[68]Duncan, L.C., Evolution of the Ambulance Corps and Field Hospital, *The Military Surgeon*, p 239.

[69]Miller, *The Photographic History of the Civil War*, Volume 7. p 280.

[70]Dammann, G.D., D.D.S., *Pictorial Encyclopedia of Civil War Medical Instruments and Equipment*, Volume 2, Missoula, MT, Pictorial Histories Publishing Co.,1988. p 26.

[71]Cunningham, *Doctors in Gray*. p 114.

[72]Ibid. p 114.

[73]Ibid. p 118.

[74]Miller, *The Photographic History of the Civil War*, Volume 7. p 282.

[75]Cunningham, *Doctors in Gray*. p 73.

[76]Ibid. p 38.

[77]Ibid. p 38.

[78]Duncan, Evolution of the Ambulance Corps and Field Hospital, *The Military Surgeon*, p 241.

[79]Adams, *Doctors in Blue*. p 119.

[80]Duncan, Evolution of the Ambulance Corps and Field Hospital, *The Military Surgeon*, p 248.

[81]Dammann, G.D., D.D.S., *Pictorial Encyclopedia of Civil War Medical Instruments and Equipment*, Volume 1, Missoula, MT, Pictorial Histories Publishing Co.,1983. p 1

[82]Smith, S., M.D., Handbook of Surgical Operations, San Francisco, CA, Norman Publishing, 1989. Reprint of 1861 original. p 10.

[83]Hamilton, F.H., M.D., *A Practical Treatise on Military Surgery*, San Francisco, CA, Norman Publishing, 1989. Reprint of 1861 original. p vii.

[84]Smith, *Hand-Book of Surgical Operations*, p 10.

[85]Tripler, C.S., M.D., and Blackman, G.C., M.D., *Hand-Book for the Military Surgeon*, Cincinnati, OH, Robert Clarke & Co., 1861. p 36.

[86]Adams, *Doctors in Blue*. p 102.

[87]Kuz, J.E., M.D., and Bengtson, B.P., M.D., *Orthopaedic Injuries of the Civil War*, Kennesaw Mountain, GA, Kennesaw Mountain Press, Inc., 1996. p 16.

[88]Adams, *Doctors in Blue*. p 103.

[89]Dammann, *Pictorial Encyclopedia of Civil War Medical Instruments and Equipment*, Volume 1. p 1.

[90]Kernek, C.B., M.D., *Field Surgeon at Gettysburg*, Indianapolis, IN, Guild Press of Indiana, Inc., 1993. p 37, 38, 57, 58, 59.

[91]Adams, Doctors in Blue. p 106.

[92]Smith, *Hand-Book of Surgical Operations*. p 92.

[93]Kuz and Bengtson, *Orthopaedic Injuries of the Civil War*. p 37.

[94]Gross, S.D., M.D., *A Manual of Military Surgery*, San Francisco, CA, Norman Publishing, 1988. Reprint of 1861 original. p 80.

[95]Smith, *Hand-Book of Surgical Operations*. p 245.

[96]Kuz and Bengtson, *Orthopaedic Injuries of the Civil War*. p 44.

[97]Ibid. Tabulated statistics from tables.

[98]Smith, *Hand-Book of Surgical Operations*. p 250.

[99]Tripler and Blackman, *Hand-Book for the Military Surgeon*. p 104.

[100]Barnes, J.K., *The Medical and Surgical History of the Civil War*, Wilmington, NC, Broadfoot Publishing Co., 1992. Reprint of 1870-1888 original.

[101]Kuz and Bengtson, *Orthopaedic Injuries of the Civil War*. p 18.

[102]Smith, *Hand-Book of Surgical Operations*. p 252.

[103]Adams, *Doctors in Blue*. p 120.

[104]Chisolm, J.J., M.D., *A Manual of Military Surgery*, San Francisco, CA, Norman Publishing, 1989. Reprint of 1861 original. p 301.

[105]Adams, *Doctors in Blue*. p 120.

[106]Roy, A., *Fallen Soldier*, Montgomery, AL, Elliot & Clark Publishing, 1996. p 33.

[107]Adams, *Doctors in Blue*. p 106.

[108]Smith, *Hand-Book of Surgical Operations*. p 245.

[109]Chisolm, *A Manual of Military Surgery*. p 138.

[110]Ibid. p 315.

[111]Smith, *Hand-Book of Surgical Operations*. p 254.

[112]Ibid. p 261.

[113]Adams, *Doctors in Blue*. p 110.

[114]Cunningham, *Doctors in Gray*. p 232.

[115]Woodward, *The Hospital Steward's Manual*. p 297.

[116]Packard, J.H., M.D., *A Manual of Minor Surgery*, San Francisco, CA, Norman Publishing, 1990. Reprint of 1863 original. p 249.

[117]Ibid. p 249.

[118]Adams, *Doctors in Blue*. p 125.

[119]Cunningham, *Doctors in Gray*. p 237.

[120]Adams, *Doctors in Blue*. p 126.

[121]Ibid. p 127.

[122]Cunningham, *Doctors in Gray*. p 240.

[123]Adams, *Doctors in Blue*. p 128.

[124]Cunningham, *Doctors in Gray*. p 234.

[125]Adams, *Doctors in Blue*. p 123.

[126]Chisolm, *A Manual of Military Surgery*. p 190.

[127]Packard, *A Manual of Minor Surgery*. p 89.

[128]Ibid. p 131.

[129]Ibid. p 191.

[130]Cunningham, *Doctors in Gray*. p 244.

[131]Ibid. p 245.

[132]Adams, *Doctors in Blue*. p 11.

[133]Barnes, *The Medical and Surgical History of the Civil War*.

[134]Woodward, J.J., M.D., *Outlines of the Chief Camp Diseases of the United States Armies*, San Francisco, CA, Norman Publishing, 1992. Reprint of 1863 original.

[135]Barnes, *The Medical and Surgical History of the Civil War*.

[136]Cunningham, *Doctors in Gray*. p 184.

[137]Woodward, *Outlines of the Chief Camp Diseases of the United States Armies*, p 11

[138]Cunningham, *Doctors in Gray.* p 163.

[139]Ibid. p 163.

[140]Hamilton, F.H., M.D., *A Practical Treatise on Military Surgery*, San Francisco, CA, Norman Publishing, 1989. Reprint of 1861 original. p 54.

[141]Ibid. p 65.

[142]Woodward, *Outlines of the Chief Camp Diseases of the United States Armies*, p 209.

[143]Adams, *Doctors in Blue.* p 172.

[144]Cunningham, *Doctors in Gray.* p 185.

[145]Dammann, *Pictorial Encyclopedia of Civil War Medical Instruments and Equipment*, Volume 1. p 44.

[146]Woodward, *Outlines of the Chief Camp Diseases of the United States Armies.* p 42.

[147]Ibid. p 32.

[148]Evans, B.A., M.D., *A Primer of Civil War Medicine*, Knoxville, TN, Bohemian Brigade Bookshop and Publishers, 1997. p 67.

[149]Adams, *Doctors in Blue.* p 196.

[150]Gross, *A Manual of Military Surgery.* p 129.

[151]Barnes, *The Medical and Surgical History of the Civil War.*

[152]Woodward, *Outlines of the Chief Camp Diseases of the United States Armies.* p 63.

[153]Barnes, *The Medical and Surgical History of the Civil War.*

[154]Gross, *A Manual of Military Surgery.* p 156.

[155]*Stedman's Medical Dictionary*, Baltimore, MD, The Williams and Wilkins Co., 1976. p 198.

[156]Wilbur, C.K., M.D., *Revolutionary Medicine 1700-1800*, Chester, CT, The Globe Pequot Press, 1980. p 9.

[157]Evans, *A Primer of Civil War Medicine.* p 1.

[158]Woodward, *Outlines of the Chief Camp Diseases of the United States Armies.* p 9.

[159]Ibid. p 11.

[160]Gross, *A Manual of Military Surgery.* p 35.

[161]Dammann, *Pictorial Encyclopedia of Civil War Medical Instruments and Equipment*, Volume 1. p 44.

[162]Evans, *A Primer of Civil War Medicine.*

[163]Cunningham, *Doctors in Gray.* p 146.

[164]Ibid. p 152.

[165]Woodward, *Outlines of the Chief Camp Diseases of the United States Armies.* p 221.

[166]Barnes, *The Medical and Surgical History of the Civil War.*

[167]*Documents of the U.S. Sanitary Commission*, 2 Volumes, New York, NY, 1866.

[168]Cunningham, *Doctors in Gray.* p 193.

[169]Lowry, T.P., M.D., *The Story the Soldiers Wouldn't Tell*, Mechanicsburg, PA, Stackpole Books, 1994. p 104.

[170]Cunningham, *Doctors in Gray.* p 211.

[171]Lowry, *The Story the Soldiers Wouldn't Tell.* p 108.

[172]Adams, *Doctors in Blue.* p 188.

[173]Cunningham, *Doctors in Gray.* p 210.

[174]Dammann, G.D., *Pictorial Encyclopedia of Civil War Medical Instruments and Equipment*, Volume 1. p 44.

[175]Gross, *A Manual of Military Surgery*. p 81.

[176]Adams, *Doctors in Blue*. p 108.

[177]Cunningham, *Doctors in Gray*. p 227.

[178]Dammann, *Pictorial Encyclopedia of Civil War Medical Instruments and Equipment*, Volume 1. p 44.

[179]*Documents of the U.S. Sanitary Commission*, 2 Volumes, New York, NY, 1866.

[180]Barnes, *The Medical and Surgical History of the Civil War*.

[181]Dammann, *Pictorial Encyclopedia of Civil War Medical Instruments and Equipment*, Volume 3., Missoula, MT, Pictorial Histories Publishing Co., Inc., 1998. p 5.

[182]Barnes, *The Medical and Surgical History of the Civil War*.

[183]Ibid.

[184]Cunningham, *Doctors in Gray*. p 145.

[185]Bollet, A.J., M.D., Lessons from Medical History-A New Look at Civil War Medicine: Introduction to a Series of Articles, *Resident and Staff Physician*, September, 1997. p 13.

- Sources of Illustrations -

Figure 1: Standard Military Issue Hand Litter - Hamilton, F.H., M.D., *A Practical Treatise on Military Surgery*, San Francisco, CA, Norman Publishing, 1989. p 125.

Figure 2: Two-Wheeled Ambulance - Hamilton, F.H., M.D., *A Practical Treatise on Military Surgery*, San Francisco, CA, Norman Publishing, 1989. p 33.

Figure 3: Four-Wheeled Ambulance - Duncan, L.C., "Evolution of the Ambulance Corps and Field Hospital," *The Military Surgeon* (March, 1913). p 240.

Figure 4: Scissors, Scalpels, Bistouries - Packard, J.H., M.D., *A Manual of Minor Surgery*, San Francisco, CA, Norman Publishing, 1990. p 11.

Figure 5: Pocket Case - Smith, S., M.D., *Hand-Book of Surgical Operations*, San Francisco, CA., Norman Publishing, 1990. p 10.

Figure 6: General Operating Case - Smith, S., M.D., *Hand-Book of Surgical Operations*, San Francisco, CA., Norman Publishing, 1990. p 11.

Figure 7: Circular Method of Amputation - Smith, S., M.D., *Hand-Book of Surgical Operations*, San Francisco, CA., Norman Publishing, 1990. p 93.

Figure 8: Flap Method of Amputation - Smith, S., M.D., *Hand-Book of Surgical Operations*, San Francisco, CA., Norman Publishing, 1990. p 158.

Figure 9: Resection - Smith, S., M.D., *Hand-Book of Surgical Operations*, San Francisco, CA., Norman Publishing, 1990. p 192.

Figure 10: Bullet Extractors - Smith, S., M.D., *Hand-Book of Surgical Operations*, San Francisco, CA., Norman Publishing, 1990. p 240, 241.

Figure 11: Trephines and Hay's Saw - Smith, S., M.D., *Hand-Book of Surgical Operations*, San Francisco, CA., Norman Publishing, 1990. p 238, 239.

Figure12: Tourniquets - Smith, S., M.D., *Hand-Book of Surgical Operations*, San Francisco, CA., Norman Publishing, 1990. p 28. and Packard, J.H., M.D., *A Manual of Minor Surgery*, San Francisco, CA, Norman Publishing, 1990. p 50.

Figure13: Instruments used to ligate vessels - Smith, S., M.D., *Hand-Book of Surgical Operations*, San Francisco, CA., Norman Publishing, 1990. p 31, 50.

Figure 14: Surgical "cut-downs" - Smith, S., M.D., *Hand-Book of Surgical Operations*, San Francisco, CA., Norman Publishing, 1990. p 54, 82.

Figure 15: "Figure-of-eight" suture technique - Smith, S., M.D., *Hand-Book of Surgical Operations*, San Francisco, CA., Norman Publishing, 1990. p 16. and Packard, J.H., M.D., *A Manual of Minor Surgery*, San Francisco, CA, Norman Publishing, 1990. p 66.

Figure 16: Serrefine - Smith, S., M.D., *Hand-Book of Surgical Operations*, San Francisco, CA., Norman Publishing, 1990. p 14.

Figure 17: Dressings - Smith, S., M.D., *Hand-Book of Surgical Operations*, San Francisco, CA., Norman Publishing, 1990. p 17. and Packard, J.H., M.D., *A Manual of Minor Surgery*, San Francisco, CA, Norman Publishing, 1990. p 111.

Figure 18: Forearm splint - Packard, J.H., M.D., *A Manual of Minor Surgery*, San Francisco, CA, Norman Publishing, 1990. p 160.

Figure 19: Fracture-box - Packard, J.H., M.D., *A Manual of Minor Surgery*, San Francisco, CA, Norman Publishing, 1990. p 186, 187.

Figure 20: Traction set-up - Packard, J.H., M.D., *A Manual of Minor Surgery*, San Francisco, CA, Norman Publishing, 1990. p 168.

Figure 21: Urinary catheter - Packard, J.H., M.D., *A Manual of Minor Surgery*, San Francisco, CA, Norman Publishing, 1990. p 219.

- BIBLIOGRAPHY and COMMENTS on SOURCES -

1. Adams, G.W., *Doctors in Blue*, New York, NY, Collier Books, 1961.
   An excellent work on the political, medical, and surgical aspects of the Union Army.

2. Barber, L.W., *Army Memoirs of Lucius Barber*, Time-Life Books, Inc., 1984.
   Reprint of 1894 original.

3. Barnes, J.K., M.D., *The Medical and Surgical History of the Civil War*, Wilmington,
   NC, Broadfoot Publishing Co., 1992.
   Reprint of *The Medical and Surgical History of the War of the Rebellion (1861-1865)*,
   published between 1870 and 1888.
   The original work was published in six massive volumes. The reprint is published in
   twelve volumes and includes the addition of three index volumes.

4. Bollet, A.J., M.D., "Lessons from Medical History-A New Look at Civil War Medicine:
   Introduction to a Series of Articles," *Resident and Staff Physician* (September, 1997).

5. Bollet, A.J., M.D., "Lessons from Medical History-Civil War Medicine: In the
   Beginning," *Resident and Staff Physician* (October, 1997).

6. Chisolm, J.J., M.D., *A Manual of Military Surgery*, San Francisco, CA, Norman
   Publishing, 1989. Reprint of 1861 original.

> Norman Publishing has reprinted twenty-three Civil War
> Era medical texts - in two series - The American Civil
> War Medical Series and The American Civil War
> Surgery Series. These reprints are of excellent quality
> and several contain original illustrations. Each book also
> includes a brief biography of the author, providing
> insight into the medical climate of the time.

7. *The Civil War CD- ROM, "The War Of the Rebellion: A Compilation of the Official
   Records of the Union and Confederate Armies,"* Carmel, IN, Guild Press of Indiana,
   Inc., 1997.
   "*The War Of the Rebellion: A Compilation of the Official Records of the Union and
   Confederate Armies*" was originally published between 1880 and 1901- in 128
   volumes - at a cost of over three million dollars. This CD-ROM includes the entire
   Official Records, as well as several other references, in an easy-to-search CD-ROM
   format. An exceptionally valuable reference tool.

8. Coggins, J., *Arms and Equipment of the Civil War*, Wilmington, NC, Broadfoot
   Publishing Co., 1962. Reprinted 1990.

9. Cunningham, H.H., *Doctors in Gray*, Baton Rouge, LA, Louisiana State University Press, 1993. The political, medical, and surgical aspects of the Confederate Army.

10. Dammann, G.D., D.D.S., *Pictorial Encyclopedia of Civil War Medical Instruments and Equipment*, Volume 1, Missoula, MT, Pictorial Histories Publishing Co., 1983.

11. Dammann, G.D., D.D.S., *Pictorial Encyclopedia of Civil War Medical Instruments and Equipment*, Volume 2, Missoula, MT, Pictorial Histories Publishing Co., 1988.

12. Dammann, G.D., D.D.S., *Pictorial Encyclopedia of Civil War Medical Instruments and Equipment*, Volume 3, Missoula, MT, Pictorial Histories Publishing Co., 1997.

> The Dammann books include dozens of photographs of Civil War era medical and surgical items. Each chapter includes an informative introduction. Excellent books.

13. Denney, R.E., *Civil War Medicine*, New York, NY, Sterling Publishing Co. Inc., 1994.
Day-by-day chronology - relating medical aspects of the Civil War - in the participants own words.

14. *The Documents of the U.S. Sanitary Commission*, 2 Volumes, New York, NY, 1866. A compilation of the ninety-five publications of the U.S. Sanitary Commission. A third volume was published in Cleveland, Ohio, in 1871, entitled: *The U.S. Sanitary Commission in the Valley of the Mississippi*, which documents the work of the Sanitary Commission in the West.

15. Duncan, L.C., "Evolution of the Ambulance Corps and Field Hospital," *The Military Surgeon* (March, 1913).

16. Duncan, L.C., "The Days Gone By - The Strange Case of Surgeon General Hammond," *The Military Surgeon* (January, 1929).

17. Evans, B.A., M.D., *A Primer of Civil War Medicine*, Knoxville, TN, Bohemian Brigade Bookshop and Publishers, 1997.
An outline of the medical (as opposed to the surgical) aspects of the Civil War.

18. Fitzpatrick, M.F., "The Mercy Brigade," *Civil War Times Illustrated* (October, 1997).

19. Gross, S.D., M.D., *A Manual of Military Surgery*, San Francisco, CA, Norman Publishing, 1988. Reprint of 1861 original.

20. Hamilton, F.H., M.D., *A Practical Treatise on Military Surgery*, San Francisco, CA, Norman Publishing, 1989. Reprint of 1862 original.

21. Kernek, C.B., M.D., *Field Surgeon at Gettysburg*, Indianapolis, IN, Guild Press of Indiana, Inc., 1993.
    A fictional account of the activities of the medical staff of the 32nd Massachusetts Regiment. Very interesting and informative reading, giving the reader the feeling of being a part of the action.

22. Kuz, J.E., M.D., and Bengston, B.P., M.D., *Orthopaedic Injuries of the Civil War*, Kennesaw Mountain, GA, Kennesaw Mountain Press, Inc., 1996.
    A pictorial atlas of orthopedic (extremity) trauma, and its surgical treatment, during the Civil War. Each chapter covers a different anatomical region. Includes numerous photographs from the original work of George A. Otis from the Army Medical Museum.

23. Lowry, T.P., M.D., *The Story the Soldiers Wouldn't Tell*, Mechanicsburg, PA, Stackpole Books, 1994.
    The sexual side of the story.

24. McHenry, R., General Editor, *The New Encyclopedia Britannica*, Chicago, IL, Encyclopedia Britannica, Inc., 1992.

25. Miller, F.T., *The Photographic History of the Civil War*, Volume 7, New York, NY, Thomas Yoseloff, Inc.,1957.
    A truly classic work. A ten volume set, originally published in 1911 - the fiftieth anniversary of the war. Available in several reprinted editions.

26. Packard, J.H., M.D., *A Manual of Minor Surgery*, San Francisco, CA, Norman Publishing, 1990. Reprint of 1863 original.

27. Roy, A., *Fallen Soldier*, Montgomery, AL, Elliot & Clark Publishing, 1996.

28. Smith, S., M.D., *Hand-Book of Surgical Operations*, San Francisco, CA., Norman Publishing, 1990. Reprint of 1862 original.

29. *Stedman's Medical Dictionary*, Baltimore, MD, The Williams and Wilkins Co., 1976.

30. Tripler, C.S., M.D., and Blackman, G.C., M.D., *Hand-Book for the Military Surgeon*, Cincinnati, OH, Robert Clarke & Co., 1861.

31. Wilbur, C.K., M.D., *Revolutionary Medicine 1700-1800*, Chester, CT, The Globe Pequot Press, 1980.

32. Woodward, J.J., M.D., *The Hospital Steward's Manual*, San Francisco, CA, Norman Publishing, 1991. Reprint of 1862 original.

33. Woodward, J.J., M.D., *Outlines of the Chief Camp Diseases of the United States Armies*, San Francisco, CA, Norman Publishing, 1992. Reprint of 1863 original.

The story of Civil War medicine is available on two VHS vidiotapes:

Between the Bullet and the Battlefield: The Truth and Myths of Civil War Medicine; New Visions Productions, Hollidaysburg, PA. 1996.

Battlefield Medicine; Time-Life Video, Alexandria, VA. 1994.

An excellent source of information regarding any aspect of Civil War medicine is:

The National Museum of Civil War Medicine
P.O. Box 470
48 E. Patrick Street
Frederick, MD   21705-0470

The Museum bookstore sells many of the above references.

- INDEX -

- About the Author -

Mark J. Schaadt, M.D. graduated in 1983 from Indiana University School of Medicine. After completing his residency in 1986, he began practicing Emergency Medicine in Quincy, Illinois. He is currently the Chairman of the Department of Emergency Medicine at Blessing Hospital in Quincy.

Mark lives in Quincy with his wife, Kristin. His interests include collecting Civil War relics and Civil War era medical antiques.